Dear Ann Volume 2:
Episodes 61-120

Letters to and from Teachers, Students, Parents, and More

By Ann Y. Mouse

Aletheia Pyralis Publishers

For information about special discounts available for bulk purchases, sales promotions, fund-raising and educational needs, please email: devyaschildren@gmail.com

http://www.juliecgilbert.com/

Love Science Fiction or Mystery?

Choose your adventure!

Visit: http://www.juliecgilbert.com/

For details on getting free books.

Dedication:

To the many teachers, parents, friends, colleagues, and random strangers who answered my many questions.

To the future teachers seeking insight or advice.

To the students we serve day in and day out.

Table of Contents:

Chapter 1:
Episode 61 – Special Guest: Lovely Art Teacher's Educational Musings Part 1

Introduction:
Dear Reader,

Our next guest has had a varied teaching career. She has taught art in an urban public school, Spanish in a private school, and art in a small homeschool group.

I mention this because every journey is unique. There's no right or wrong way to end up as a teacher. Sometimes, the calling lasts a lifetime, and sometimes, it makes up only one season of life.

Since most of her experience has been with art, I shall refer to this guest as the Lovely Art Teacher. (Mostly because she is lovely and still does a lot of art, but also because Former Art Teacher has an unfortunate acronym.)

~Ann

Note: The teacher's formal school experiences happened in the pre-pandemic era. I haven't gotten to discuss the impacts of that yet, but it is good to keep in mind as we hear what the Lovely Art Teacher has to say.

First up, some background.

Why did you become a teacher?

Lovely Art Teacher: I thought teaching would make me a successful person.

How did you become a teacher?

Lovely Art Teacher: I applied to and got accepted into an alternate route program for an urban school district.

It consisted of a summer crash course in teaching and twice monthly meetings throughout the first year.

How long did you stay in that district?

Lovely Art Teacher: I was there 2 years.

How were the kids in your art classes?

Lovely Art Teacher: Children emulate the people around them.
I had many good experiences because most kids love art.
Still, I had a few problem kids who created chaos. There were middle school students integrated into the elementary school. I'd say from 5th grade up, the kids' behavior got worse.

Why did you leave your first teaching job?

Lovely Art Teacher: So many reasons.
First, it was a terrible working environment.
- Other teachers were leaving.
- The children barely did any work.
- The kids were acting out.
- When I spoke to the union people, they said I could file a discrimination complaint and that's about it.

- The school was a wreck. There was graffiti everywhere because kids were rebelling against the principal's beautification projects. They even used gang like symbols as a scare tactic against the adults. We're talking 3rd grade kids and up to about 5th.

More personally, I was put on a *rescue plan*, which is essentially the school saying you're a terrible teacher. That's really hard on the ego.

The biggest issue by far though happened to be that the principal at the time was an incompetent wreck.

Me: Ah, yes. I believe I had something similar happen to me my first year of teaching. I came close to quitting but ended up in a much better job situation at a different school.

Administration can indeed make or break a teaching situation. Do you think there are other factors to teacher retention or student success?

Lovely Art Teacher: Student success has a lot to do with the parenting (or lack thereof).

There was a distinct lack of support from parents. Many of them lived at the poverty level. They worked multiple jobs. They didn't have the time, energy, or knowledge how to parent well.

I was told that teachers not from the area would be considered outsiders, and that I shouldn't take it personally. But it's really difficult not to take something like that personally.

What other formal teaching experiences have you had?

Lovely Art Teacher: I had the chance to be a maternity leave substitute teacher for a Spanish class in a Catholic high school. That was a great experience.

I also got to teach art to a small group of children. We met in a library. I believe they were part of a Montessori school, so the kids ranged a bit in ages. That too, was an excellent experience. I still miss those kids to this day.

You've already told us that unsupportive (and sometimes overbearing) administration ended your first teaching experience. What happened with the other teaching experiences?

Lovely Art Teacher: The Spanish teaching position was always going to be temporary. The regular teacher had her baby and returned.

Around that time, I was about to get married, so there were a lot of wedding planning details to attend to.

Since I was getting some freelance art jobs, I decided to move my career in that direction. One of my colleagues at that first job stayed on because she needed the job to stay in the country. She was also an aide, so she had less kids to work with in that hostile environment. I had other options, so I took them.

Do you know what happened in your old urban district?

Lovely Art Teacher: I think it's better now.

Two months after I quit, one of the computer teachers kicked up a huge fuss. The kids were out of control. He'd been letting the kids just play and not teaching them anything because they were destroying the computers. After he got fired, he used his union connections to get some changes made.

There was also another teacher with connections to television. She showed off the disaster that was happening. Eventually, the district restructured the schools to remove the middle school students from that building.

Incidentally, I learned that I could have my old job back if I wanted it, but once I learned that it would be with the same terrible principal, I told them no way. (I will not work with that woman. She's a disaster.)

Hindsight is perfect. I later found out that the terrible principal failed to meet her goals for the school, and the district returned her to her old job.

This is a good stopping point.

We're about half-way through. Next up, I'd love to dive deeper into the tough teaching experience.

Takeaways:
- Parents are vital to the learning equation.
- Supportive administrators are also important.
- Every teaching position is different.
- Some people are driven from teaching by circumstances. Some choose to leave (or stay away). Our guest had some of both experiences.

Chapter 2:
Episode 62 – Special Guest: Lovely Art Teacher's Educational Musings Part 2

Introduction:
Dear Reader,

Let's dig a little deeper into the heartbreaking story being played out all over the country.

These exact events happened over a decade ago, but they're still relevant today.

~Ann

You mentioned your first teaching experience (which lasted two years) was sort of crazy. Can you elaborate on that?
Lovely Art Teacher: These are some of the problems I had.
- Some kids sort of stalked me. – That made me feel uncomfortable, so I started locking my door on off periods. This annoyed some of my colleagues.
- The kids acted out.

- My cell phone was stolen.
- Kids made obscene gestures.
- Kids got into fights with each other.
- The students broke chairs and tables.
- Some students broke art supplies on purpose.
- Kids screamed at random and stepped out of the classroom whenever they felt like it.

Wow, that's a lot of violence. What do you think caused or made the problems worse?

Lovely Art Teacher: Unfortunately, these kids witnessed a lot of violence at home. They also had a hard time focusing on school stuff because of their broken homes. Parents didn't show up for conferences about behavior.

The kids weren't taught how to behave in an art class. They didn't think that art mattered to their lives. It can be something that enhances life, but they didn't get that part because nobody previously had emphasized it.

What did you do to try to motivate your students to do the lessons?

Lovely Art Teacher: I implemented a reward system that included fun erasers, pencils, candy, and other small items. I even bargained with free time. I bought something every morning. Since the kids didn't care to learn for intrinsic reasons, I made a deal they understood.

The principal (and some of my colleagues) hated the reward system, so she told me I couldn't use it anymore. The kids were also angry because some other teachers took the rewards away and would only return them if they also behaved in their classes.

The jealous ones would say that I used the reward system because I had no classroom management skills. They didn't get that they taught practical stuff, things that the kids understand (or were repeatedly told) had life value.

What did the terrible principal do (or not do) that made the situation worse?

Lovely Art Teacher:
- She killed my reward system.
- She would get to school really late and leave early.
- She broke up some of the extracurricular activities.
- She canceled a field trip the kids were excited about.
- She monitored me excessively just to *keep me on my toes*.
- She told us that referrals should only be for fighting, not playful fighting.

Buy-in from the kids is important. Want to talk about that?

Lovely Art Teacher: When I did a year-long maternity leave teaching Spanish at a Catholic school, I worked with high school students who had been raised very differently than the elementary kids at the urban school.

It wasn't perfect. I still had some problem students, but for the most part, I was able to dive deep into the material and build a great rapport with the kids.

This school supported them very well. It had normal class for four days. The fifth day of the week was for skills. They even had an after-school program just for homework.

Those kids were very prepared for college, and they had a safe environment to learn in.

Tell me about the day you quit the first job.

Lovely Art Teacher: I was teaching a 5th grade class, and they were getting out of hand. I couldn't call for help.

The troublemaking students were very frank with me. They said they were acting out because they hated the principal and wanted to get rid of her. They also knew that the teachers weren't getting support.

All my annual reports were satisfactory, but I couldn't stand to be in that environment any longer.

What about that little homeschooling experience you mentioned? Can you tell us about that?

Lovely Art Teacher: I did that for a year and a half to two years. It was an awesome experience but the drive down to the location was over an hour.

The small group of kids I taught art to had a similar skill level. I got to explore different kinds of art with them. They especially loved learning about comics.

It was excellent in part because the kids wanted to be there. Also, we met in a library, so the kids had to be calm to learn in that environment.

Do you do any teaching alongside your current work?

Lovely Art Teacher: I do freelance art now. I have done some live streams for fans. That's an informal kind of teaching where I'll go through my techniques to accomplish something. They're eager to learn.

What were the best, worst, and most fun portions of traditional teaching?

Lovely Art Teacher:

- **Best and most fun part:** I loved the give and take of teaching and learning. The ah-ha moment where the kids trusted the art lesson enough to apply it and truly get it and make something wonderful.
- **Worst:** Working for a terrible principal. People who don't know how to support the teachers create an environment that becomes unsafe. (You don't have to enable incompetence, but teachers need support.)

What do you think went wrong at your first school district?

Lovely Art Teacher: There's a vicious cycle. The parents in that district worked two to three jobs. They struggled with bills and such and didn't really have the time to be good parents. They depended on the school to fill that gap.

The school district didn't have the resources (money, time, and leadership with a vision) to implement the kinds of programs the students needed to succeed.

What do you think kids need to succeed at school?

- Support
- After school program with homework help
- Life skills: How to manage an agenda, do presentations, get a job
- Kids need to be taught how to be people. There's more to life than book knowledge.

It got to the point that when kids spent more time at home like over the summer, they went backwards emotionally. We ended up teaching them social norms.

Me: I teach in a high school. Many students mature a lot over the summers, but I think I also work in a different world than Lovely Art Teacher's urban experience.

Lovely Art Teacher: Kids imitate what's around them, so when they immerse themselves in social media, bad habits ensue.

That's an interesting point. What do you think some of the social media dangers include?

- An uptick in narcissistic tendencies.
- Heightened sense of entitlement – Kids argue over stupid stuff.

- Isolation leads people to gather in like-minded groups that tell you what you want to hear. There's no incentive to grow and learn from others.

Thank you for sharing. Do you have anything you'd like to say to parents?

I heard one of my former students ended up getting into trouble later in life. That's sad. I feel bad because I know the kid made terrible choices, but he also didn't get the support he needed to develop a good character (and make better life choices).

To parents: You have to be involved in your children's lives. Show that you care about them. It's not about buying things. It's about investing in their lives, checking homework, and hanging out with them. Your decisions affect them in so many ways. To bring a kid into the world, you need the room for them. That includes time, money, and emotional energy to invest in them.

Takeaways:

- Parents need to be involved in their kids' lives.
- When students want to be there, learning happens.

Chapter 3:
Episode 63 – Special Guest: Former Private School Elementary Teacher (K,2)

Introduction:
Dear Reader,

Everybody's life journey is different.

Some people's path (like mine) sends them into many different teaching experiences for the bulk of their career.

Others only take up the mantel for a short time. This can be for a variety of reasons.

There's nothing wrong with teaching for a short time. The cool thing about elementary school is that you get to be with those kids a whole lot for that year you work with them.

~Ann

Note: I'm going to use Former K, 2 Teacher as my title for this wonderful guest because it's a lot easier than saying Private School Elementary Teacher with experience in Kindergarten and Second

Grade.

Hi. Thanks for chatting with me. Glad our schedules finally worked out. Tell me about your teaching experiences.

How many years did you teach?
Former K, 2 Teacher: I did my student teaching in an urban third grade classroom. My other two years were in a Quaker school working in kindergarten and second grade.

I also did a little subbing, but I didn't like it. The life was too nomadic, unsteady, and stressful. I couldn't form connections with any of the kids.

Let's talk a bit about that student teaching experience. How did that go?
Former K, 2 Teacher: Bad. It was a summer intensive program in an urban area.

What made it difficult?
Former K, 2 Teacher: So many reasons really.
- The families were poor, and many of the families were broken.
- The kids were emotional messes.
- None of the technology worked. (And I mean none.)
- It was a zoo. There were lots of behavioral issues, and I couldn't even lay sole blame on the kids.
- The classroom was rundown and breaking down.
- Textbooks were old.

That kind of environment made it difficult for the kids to cope, let alone learn.

Why did you become a teacher?
Former K, 2 Teacher: I wanted to interact with young kids, get to know them, and inspire them.

Once you got your regular teaching job, what was that like? Tell us about the school.

Former K, 2 Teacher: I worked in a small Quaker school. The value and community aspects of that private school were great.

How long did it take you to prepare for class?

Former K, 2 Teacher: All Saturday, most Saturdays.

How did you approach prep?

Former K, 2 Teacher: The school had pretty good collaboration between staff. We had biweekly meetings and a distinct curriculum to follow. I built my plans around that.

Having taught kindergarten and second grade, which did you enjoy more?

Former K, 2 Teacher: I enjoyed teaching second grade more than kindergarten because they're doing more in general, especially reading. Kindergarten tended to have a much bigger focus on play, so it turned more into a crowd control job. I found kindergarten more challenging. It was like pulling teeth.

Did you have a favorite topic to teach?

Former K, 2 Teacher: Writing to second graders. It involved a lot of journal entries and writing reflections. I liked the imaginative writing sections. I would give the students writing prompts and see what they could come up with. They even had a larger storybook project that got presented to their peers and parents.

Close seconds would be history and science.

The science involved a lot of exploring a nearby creek, making observations, gathering soil samples, and going on nature hikes. This tied back into writing because the students would then journal about the experience.

What was your least favorite topic to teach?

Former K, 2 Teacher (in about a quarter of a second): Math. It wasn't normal math. There was some weird way of doing things that I had to learn separately in order to teach it.

We've talked topics. Let's step back and consider broader for a moment. What are the best, worst, and most fun parts of teaching?

Former K, 2 Teacher:

- Best part – Seeing relationships grow between kids.
- Worst part – If you have problem kids, you're stuck with them. (On the plus side, because it was a private school and parents had to pay to send their kids there, the parents generally backed the teachers.)
- Most fun part – Seeing the students' final writing projects and sharing the results with parents carried a large sense of accomplishment for me and the students.

Did you have any problems with kids?

Former K, 2 Teacher: Absolutely. Some were stubborn and determined to do their own thing. This made them poor direction followers and disruptive in general.

Being dominant in one's family is one thing, but that doesn't always translate well to a school setting. That's difficult to bring up in a parent conference. I usually tried to phrase it as the kid has *unused leadership potential*.

Would you consider working in a public school?

Former K, 2 Teacher: Not really. Many of my colleagues in the private school had worked in a public school. The way they talked about administration sort of scared me off from seeking a job there.

Would you ever consider teaching again?

Former K, 2 Teacher: No. I love the regular hours of my office job. School was emotionally taxing. There's an emotional cost that's particularly high when you're an introvert working in a school.

The prep and grading weighed on me, and the finances weren't working out favorably.

Teaching is a life calling. Some of the boundaries get blurry. You get to ingrain a love of learning in young people, take an interest in—and invest in—their lives through attending extracurricular activities.

The corporate world has better boundaries, but I do sometimes miss teaching.

Do you have any advice to new teachers?
Former K, 2 Teacher: Teach for the right reasons: the kids. Making sure you instill a love of learning, curiosity, and a love for each other.

Teach them that it's not about the grade.

When do you think the obsession for grades kicks in?
Former K, 2 Teacher: Probably the end of second grade.

What do kids need to succeed at school? (Takeaways)
Former K, 2 Teacher:
- Social skills – how to get along
- Communication skills – how to ask for help
- Supportive parents – they are a huge influence on a kid
- Self-advocacy – finding one's voice isn't just about answering questions

Chapter 4:
Episode 64 – Special Guest: Former Program Worker for Before and After School Care

Introduction:

Dear Reader,

I'll be honest. This one never even crossed my mind to seek out. I guess it's just one of those underappreciated jobs like being a janitor or a buildings and grounds worker. (Those are on the mental check list of people to track down, so please let me know if you know somebody. I'd love to interview them.)

One reason for this might be that my experience has been at a high school and these programs are rarer at this level. The school opens a little before it's set to start, and students can wait in the gym or cafeteria. After school, they catch a bus, walk, or stick around for an extracurricular thing.

Many people have to work beyond the normal school operating hours, so before and after school programs are quite popular in both public and private schools.

I feel kind of bad for the kids who have to do either, but the sympathy is compounded for those who need to do both. That's a lot of time in one place.

Being a curious soul, I looked up how much before and after school care costs. According to Google, it can range from a hundred to almost eight hundred dollars per month.

Yikes. Kids are expensive.

~Ann

Note: I'm going to use Former Care Worker as the tag because Before School and After School Care Program Worker is a little too clunky for my tastes.

How much did you earn working at the before and after school care programs?

Former Care Worker: I earned around $11-$12 per hour. Once, I got paid overtime ($20) because I had to stay with a student whose mom got stuck in traffic.

Me: That makes sense. Never thought about it, but I guess after school care isn't exactly a job where you can clock out if there's still a kid waiting to be picked up.

Disclaimer: The hourly wage quoted here is likely outdated since this person's job experience happened several years ago.

What times did the programs run?

Former Care Worker: The after-school program ran from 3:30 to 6:00 p.m., and the morning program ran for about an hour before school.

How many kids participated in the programs?

Former Care Worker: It varied day to day, but generally, there were five staff members working to watch over 50-60 kids. I think the state had a requirement of one staff member per ten kids.

Me: I was going to say I couldn't imagine that many kids at once in one space, but then, I remembered lunch duties can be one staffer to that many or more kids this year. It's a different scenario because these kids are older, but still, even with good kids, there's a lot of activity going on when you pack that many people in.

Did you enjoy the work?
Former Care Worker: Yes, but it's physically and mentally exhausting work.

Me: I can imagine. Even easy days of teaching can be draining in multiple ways.

Were the kids well-behaved?
Former Care Worker: Most of the kids were good, but of course, there were some disruptive ones in the mix as well. After being in school all day, many had a lot of energy to expend.

Were the programs structured or did you let the kids run free?
Former Care Worker: Some of both.

There was more structure involved in afternoon care. Sign-in could take 15-20 minutes, depending on how many kids showed up that day. We had a homework club, playground, snacks, and a special activity, which involved arts and crafts. The children chose which they wanted to participate in.

Morning care was more apt to be glorified babysitting. It was much quieter because less kids attended morning care. I suppose the tradeoff came in the form of the snack being more of an actual breakfast, which was harder to clean up.

Did you get to know any of the kids?
Former Care Worker: Some. There were kids who attended both programs regularly. I even got some tutoring gigs out of those connections.

Oh, and what was the going rate for tutoring?
Former Care Worker: $15/hour

Me: *Nearly chokes* Maybe I've been spoiled, but I probably wouldn't tutor for that price, but then again, it was ages ago. Maybe the equivalent rate modified for inflation would be more acceptable.

Why did you stop working that job?
Former Care Worker: I quit mainly for financial reasons. It was costing me too much money to drive back and forth for the few hours of work I got. I needed a steady, full-time job to pay my bills.

Takeaways:
- Before and after school care programs are necessary for many parents who don't have the luxury of leaving their kids with friends, a nanny, or grandparents.
- These programs can be expensive.
- The care workers don't necessarily get paid very well, but the hours are regular because there's always a demand.

Chapter 5:
Episode 65 – Special Guest: Former Immigrant Student (Brave Former Student)

Introduction:

Dear Reader,

Do you have any idea how difficult it is to track down former students?

You'd think that would be the easiest category of guest to track down since presumably everybody has been a student of some kind once upon a time.

The truth is that many people have difficult school experiences and would just like to forget that time. As such, talking about high school may not top their list of favorite things to do.

~Ann

Note: I'm going to go with Brave Former Student as my title because of the people I've asked, this is only the second person willing to talk about their high school days. (Getting teachers to talk to me is much easier. Apparently, we're an opinionated lot.)

When did you come to the United States?
Brave Former Student: I was seven, and my brother was two.

Did you enjoy high school?
Brave Former Student: No, I did not like high school. The social aspects were okay, but my home life was stressful. My parents didn't really speak English, so they couldn't help with any of the work.

I played the good student game for a while, but by the time I reached eleventh grade, I was just done with the game.

Did you have friends in high school?
Brave Former Student: Yes. We were pretty close and stayed in touch until college.

Was any part of high school fun?
Brave Former Student: I liked my music classes. I was in the choir and the band (flute player).

What made high school difficult from the homefront?
Brave Former Student:
- I didn't have my own space.
- My family was low middle class, so we lived in a tiny, run-down house.
- My folks had a language barrier they never overcame. Instead, they would ask me to ask the landlord to do this or that. It was a lot of extra pressure.
- I didn't stand up to my parents over the extra responsibilities.

How did you handle the pressures of high school?
Brave Former Student: By twelfth grade even music classes didn't cut it as an escape for me.

I felt trapped.

Home wasn't emotionally safe, and my parents wouldn't let me get a job.

I became truant and walked to the public library because I didn't have a car or any money to get further.

Somehow, I stayed out of the crowd that likes to do drugs, but I was still lost in many ways.

Do you have any high school regrets?
Brave Former Student:
- I wish I had studied harder and gotten into a better college.
- I wish I had gotten closer to some of the teachers and learned to reach out to them.
- I didn't have the words to know I was dealing with mental health stuff and had depression.
- I got very good at hiding the issues, but by the third and fourth marking period of Senior year everything crashed and burned.

Me: Nobody knew because that kind of burnout gets hidden behind general senioritis.
- This one is more general, but I wish schools were better at mental health care. Kids need a safe place to go to get mental health support.

Me: I think there is a much greater emphasis on this today, but success is going to vary widely.

Was college a better experience?
Brave Former Student: Yes. College was better overall. My freshman year was very rough, but then, I found direction.

What got better?
Brave Former Student:
- My faith got stronger.
- I found older adults who cared enough to mentor me.
- I gained focus, life direction, and meaning.
- The distance from my parents did a lot of good.
- I had a job and some money.
- I learned to set up boundaries and have a life outside of my parents' influence.

What life lessons have you learned? What would you like to pass on to the next generation of students? (Quite a few Takeaways)
Brave Former Student:
- I resented my parents for comparing me to other immigrant kids. (This person does this or that person got that scholarship.)
- I resented my parents for not overcoming their own troubles. Instead of dealing with things, they checked out and left the problems to others to solve.
- I was a quitter.
- I used to have a victim mentality.
- I used to blame circumstances for my troubles.
- I didn't know how to be resilient.
- I let learned helplessness creep in and control parts of my life.
- Make the most of opportunities you have.
- I complained a lot about what I didn't have, and that led me to not enjoy what I did have.
- I didn't know I could talk to teachers. It was difficult to articulate that I wasn't doing homework because I was lazy. I was depressed.

- I eventually found a road to forgiveness where my parents are concerned. I learned to be compassionate and not judge them. I can finally see them as flawed people, and I finally got to mourn the mother-daughter relationship I longed for but never got.
- Use the resources you have. My school days were before internet searches became so easy.
- When I got to college, mental health services were free. Help is out there if you can work up the energy to seek it.

My response:
This is the perfect example of hindsight being a heck of a lot clearer than the moment. I'm glad Brave Former Student found her way, and hope others can draw inspiration from hearing her story. That sort of history is hard-fought. It would be a shame to waste the valuable life lessons.

Chapter 6:
Episode 66 – Special Guest: Former Computer Teacher Part 1 – Background

Introduction:

Dear Reader,

Everybody answers questions differently.

Sometimes, I get one-word answers or a few sentences, and sometimes, I get storytime.

I love the differences, for they can tell us almost as much about the speakers as the words of wisdom they give us.

This is going to be a storytime. I'll break it into logical chunks so we can process properly.

~Ann

How many years did you teach?

Former Computer Teacher: The answer depends on how you define teaching.

I spent twenty-three years at a small Christian school. Much of that was full-time, but I scaled back to thirty hours a week after my grandson's birth.

Beyond that, I spent many years volunteering to teach Sunday School and Vacation Bible School programs.

Have you ever coached anything?

Former Computer Teacher: Yes. I coached the school's First Tech Challenge Robotics team from 2009 to 2017. That met two nights per week plus Saturday morning during the competition season.

Did you always know you wanted to be a teacher?

Former Computer Teacher: Yes, again. I would have told you at eight years old that I wanted to be a teacher when I grew up. I adored my K-3 teachers, and they inspired me to love learning from that time forth.

Tell us about your early years. Did you have friends in high school?

Former Computer Teacher: I was born in Vermont in 1955 and had a wonderfully rich early childhood with doting parents and inspiring teachers. (I was an only child until the age of eight.)

I knew all about the Trojan War and Queen Helen because we would build the infamous horse with tables and blankets and act it out. I could recognize and name all the instruments in Prokofiev's opera, *Peter and the Wolf*, because that was the music that accompanied snack time.

I spent most of my time outside camping, hiking, cycling, swimming, and skating with my many school and neighborhood friends.

And then, the summer before fourth grade, a lot of things changed. I moved across the Connecticut River into a very small and closed New Hampshire town because my parents were attracted by the lower taxes and the ability to own their own home.

The changes:
- The schools were different.
- I had a male teacher.
- The townspeople seemed not so friendly to a scared nine-year-old.
- I got a new baby brother!

I lived across the cornfield from the elementary school and was allowed to go home for lunch. I crossed that field at noonday for three years sometimes crying and sometimes talking to God.

I never really did fit in. I suppose the same was true for my parents, but I didn't understand that at the time.

Eventually I found my niche in being a good student, one of only a few preparing for college in my class of thirty-nine students.

The teachers liked me well enough, and I had a couple classmates and a neighbor girl whom I counted as friends.

I actually preferred spending my time alone, mostly reading. I also looked after my brother especially when he began kindergarten.

Did you get close to any teachers when you were a student?
Former Computer Teacher: My teachers affected me greatly, both positively and negatively, especially since my confidence and self-esteem at that time were based largely on my academic performance.

Because my school was very small, I knew all the teachers, but I only studied under those few in the college prep track. Most of my peers were following the business or general ed curricula.

Mini-Teacher Reports:

- My advanced math teacher encouraged me greatly and invited me back to speak to his classes when I was home from college.
- My band director was a constant source of encouragement and I even considered majoring in music because of his influence.
- My PE teacher used to make jokes about the students who weren't strong athletes.
- I refused to take Driver's Ed in school because the instructor, who also taught geometry, was teasing and unpleasant. (Ironically, my brother ended up marrying his daughter!)

As I grew wiser, I realized that perceptions of my former teachers were not always accurate. This alerted me to how my own actions and reactions as a teacher affected my students' perceptions of me and what I wanted those perceptions to be.

Have you always been a teacher, or did you have a different career?

Former Computer Teacher: Although I wanted to be a teacher throughout my childhood and into my teens, my parents and guidance counselors advised against it.

At that time in the 1970s, there was a glut of teachers and jobs were scarce.

What got you into tech education?

Former Computer Teacher: Technology education was new, and when a representative from Wang Computers visited my high school with an "amazing" machine that could solve a math problem entered in on a punched card, I was hooked.

I learned the BASIC programming language and began to consider a career in computer science.

Soon after I graduated from Rochester Institute of Technology with a Bachelor of Science in Computer Science, I jumped in and got a Master of Science in Computer Science from Rutgers University.

I worked as a computer programmer until the birth of my first child. From then until I began my official teaching job at the private school, my career involved being Mommy to my four lovely children. The career came with a lot of volunteer work that accompanied their activities and schooling.

During those intervening seventeen years, the technology field continued to develop without me and when I felt I was ready to reenter the workforce, I didn't even know what *Windows* or the *World Wide Web* was!

Me: That's a perfect stopping point. I have so many more questions, but you've already given us a lot to ponder.

Takeaways:
- Everybody has a niche.
- Technology changes swiftly.
- The number of teaching jobs ebbs and flows.
- Teacher perceptions and kid perceptions may differ.
- Change is a part of life. Change can be hard, but it can also be good.

Chapter 7:
Episode 67 – Special Guest: Former Computer Teacher Part 2 – School Preparation

Introduction:

Dear Reader,

If anybody could teach lessons on how to prepare for a wide variety of classes, I have no doubt it's our current guest.

She has had a lot of practice at it.

Spoiler: She regularly had five different classes to prepare lesson plans for. Even if they only took an hour to prepare for the week, that's a tremendous amount of work.

We can get into more of a lengthy discussion about the unpaid overtime that comes with the teaching job later. For now, let's get back to hearing from our guest.

~Ann

Before we jump back into teaching questions, were you involved in extracurriculars when you were a student?

Former Computer Teacher: I was active in the school band and was editor of the high school yearbook before the advent of computers in schools.

Back in my day, in my small hometown, if you didn't play sports, there wasn't much else to do. I did join the basketball team one season, when girls' teams played with six members on the floor. I think I only scored one basket that year.

If our school had had an archery team, I would have joined. It was my favorite rotation in Physical Education class, and I wasn't too bad at it.

Okay, back on track for some education questions. Why did you choose teaching?

Former Computer Teacher: I chose teaching because I love to learn myself and because I had wonderful examples in early childhood and throughout my formative years.

I was probably obnoxious to many of my friends in my tween years because, when we got together, I wanted to play *school.* I had workbooks and made-up assignments and gave grades!

Me: Oh, yeah, definitely something teacher lifers do. Your poor friends. Though there is something magical about work that doesn't really count.

Later, after volunteer work in Head Start, Sunday School, VBS, etc., I realized how much I loved helping a little person—especially an enthusiastic one—learn and master something for the first time.

I was always good at speaking with young children, and they seemed to like me better than my peers. I still do well with older folks (even though I'm one myself now) and kids. It's with my peers where communication has always been more difficult.

Teaching was also a natural move after spending 17 years out of the workforce. I was too rusty to make the move back into a technical field, but I could return to my first love and be on the same schedule as my own children.

Was teaching your first career?

Former Computer Teacher: I began at a communications company as a computer programmer. I never was formally educated for a career in teaching but received certification while on the job.

What kind of school did you work in?

Former Computer Teacher: I taught in a private, non-denominational, parent-run, Christian school, currently pre-K to twelfth grade that has existed for almost 75 years.

What classes did you teach?

Former Computer Teacher: The curriculum changed over the years, but basically, I taught all of the high school computer classes including applications, basic programming languages and concepts, and the two Advanced Placement Computer Science courses.

I also taught the middle school introduction to computers including applications, programming, and robotics.

What was the most preps you had in a year?

Former Computer Teacher: Probably seven or eight, but they weren't all every day. I think, for the most part, I taught five different courses every day for most of my time at that school. This continued even when I went part-time.

Many days I had no prep periods at all, although I was relieved from study halls and lunch duty.

Me: I think the most I've ever had was three preps (classes to prepare lesson plans for), and that was daunting. I legitimately get chills thinking of seven to eight preps.

How long did it take you to prepare for your classes?

Former Computer Teacher: Weekly prep for five different classes a day is time-consuming.

I spent probably one to two hours a night and a few hours on the weekend getting things organized in the form required by the administration.

My prep was always more detailed than required, but that helped me stay on track during the class period. I never repeated the same lesson in a given day, so I had to be able to move quickly from one subject—and sometimes room—to another.

I seldom was able to accomplish prep work during the school day especially after I switched to part-time.

Most of the time, students looked for help in the computer lab during my prep times or I was busy working on maintaining the computers in the lab.

How did you approach prep?

Former Computer Teacher: I think about what I want all students to achieve by the end of a unit and gear my lessons to that goal. I informally assess after almost every lesson and at regular intervals.

Whenever possible I used project-based instruction, using the first lesson in a unit to present the project and assuring the students that they will complete the project gradually as they learn the required material.

I wanted the students to be aware of the objective of each lesson. I made rubrics available for most formally assessed work.

Standards were important to me in that they affected how a particular assignment was constructed and justified the anticipated outcomes.

Above all, I taught with questions. I included as many questions as I could think of in my lesson plans.

I outlined units in advance, but I didn't complete the actual prep more than one to two weeks in advance. That was long enough so I didn't panic the night before a lesson, but short enough that I could be flexible and modify lessons when necessary to meet the class's needs.

Even after teaching the same subject for many years, class needs differed, and I would like to think that I was mostly responsive to that.

Takeaways:
- Preparing for classes is usually done best within a limited timespan, like 1-3 weeks.
- Questions are at the heart of teaching.
- Rubrics are helpful for students and teachers.
- Teachers don't typically hide what's expected of the students for a particular project.

Chapter 8:
Episode 68 – Special Guest: Former Computer Teacher Part 3 – Best and Worst

Introduction:

Dear Reader,

Lots of great tidbits to come.

I'll let the guest do the talking.

~Ann

What was your favorite class to teach?

Former Computer Teacher: My favorite class was Advanced Placement (AP) Computer Science because the students were at a higher level and really wanted to be there.

I also greatly enjoyed the beginning computer class because of the joy that some of the students found when they could go beyond just playing with the computer for entertainment and create something interesting themselves.

I never had much problem with motivation in the AP class, although some students realized very quickly that they had no interest in the subject and turnover in the first three weeks of school was usually extensive.

This is the primary reason I pushed to have programming classes introduced in the middle school so that the students would know if they wanted to follow the computer track in high school.

What was your favorite topic to teach?

Former Computer Teacher: I loved to teach computer programming. More specifically, I loved conveying the logic and abstraction that make a programmer successful.

I love to listen to students' ideas, and I have learned much from them over the years.

What was your least favorite class to teach?

Former Computer Teacher: Any middle school class because of the drama, especially among the girls.

One time I was tasked with substituting in middle school band. The students had been previously instructed to break into groups and practice their assigned songs, so I expected some talking and excess noise.

They tired of that pretty quickly and convinced me to allow them to try the piece in unison with a student conductor. So, I chose a responsible conductor, but apparently, I didn't understand that at least one student was also allowed to stand in front as if playing a solo.

Soon, almost everyone came up to the front to solo, the conductor was directing almost empty chairs, the cacophony was overwhelming, I had totally lost control, and forty minutes never stretched on so long!

It also seems that whenever I subbed in a middle school class, someone was either crying or had to go see the guidance counselor right away!

Me: This is precisely why I do not teach middle school. God bless those who do.

What is the best part of teaching?

Former Computer Teacher: The best part of teaching is getting to know some of the students as individuals and being a trustworthy mentor. Often this relationship involves the families and extends appropriately outside of school and beyond.

- I have been invited to Eagle Scout ceremonies, weddings, musical performances, plays, and more.
- Alumni from my first year of teaching still correspond with me, and I hope that I can offer them encouragement and sound advice when asked.
- Making a difference in the lives of students, praying for them, and watching them—and now, some of their children—soar are wonderful blessings from God.
- I smile whenever a student accidentally calls me *Mom*. Partnering with parents and filling in for them when they cannot be there is a solemn responsibility.

I may be a little strange in this way, but I also loved parent-teacher conferences because they were a wonderful way to get to understand the student.

If given the chance, I would always sit with parents, rather than colleagues, at school activities. Maybe it's because I identify better as a parent having raised four kids myself, or maybe it's because I prefer to talk about family stuff rather than school stuff.

What is the worst part of teaching?

Former Computer Teacher: I have never enjoyed subjective grading and am somewhat suspicious of objective grading.

On one hand, I understand that objective grading as a predictor of standardized tests results and future success in college/career is useful and often motivating, and generally, I am in favor of standards.

On the other hand, I have seen enough students fail to know that success on standardized tests is not always, or even often, the best predictor of what that student actually knows and has to offer.

So, I don't really like giving multiple-choice tests, yet I have to prepare them for what to expect further on in their academic studies.

For subjective grading ...
- I tried to always use rubrics as a learning tool for the student and to justify my grades, especially, and often, to the parents.
- I make lots of comments.
- I have to decide whether to let a student redo an assignment or retake a test.
- I have to consider how fair this is to the rest of the class.

To me, being fair is important but often hard, and I know that students can take advantage of my indecisiveness about it.

The conundrum:
- I never want to train them to not do their best work the first time, but I don't want to punish those who really are trying.
- I can't make extra credit available to some and not others.

The whole class grading is just a headache for me.
I am sure that I would make a much better tutor than classroom educator preferring to zone in on each student's gifts/talents/delights and mentoring them accordingly, even if it differs from how I might mentor and grade another student.

When do you think the emphasis on grades kicks in?
Former Computer Teacher: I understand the importance of

giving students and their parents a realistic picture of progress expected at each level.

I do believe in competition as a motivator for everyone, but at the same time I also believe in having enough activities so that everyone has a chance to *win* at something.

I don't like the idea of labeling kids as *slow* early or passing every student through as outstanding.

Since our academic system is built upon grades (somewhat inflated, I think), probably introducing grades at the beginning of middle school would be sufficient with earlier "grades" based on a rubric of skills that are recorded as partially or fully mastered.

I have taught many students who obsessed over grades. Fear of a lower grade sometimes prevents students from attempting harder work which may be interesting or beneficial to them.

I think students who prioritize learning over grades are happier, for it gives them confidence to strive for things later in life that they may perceive as too difficult.

What is the most fun part of teaching?

Former Computer Teacher: I have always enjoyed being a class advisor and working with students from the beginning to end of high school.

I enjoy planning events, going on trips, overseeing service opportunities, and watching for the gifts and talents of even the quieter ones to emerge.

It gives me a much broader appreciation for the depth of character in the class and a better understanding and appreciation of each of the students. It gives me a chance to serve all of them (not just the ones I teach everyday) and to try to earn their respect.

Takeaways:

- Middle school is a rough time.
- Grading accurately but fairly is difficult.
- Connections make teaching fun.

Chapter 9:
Episode 69 – Special Guest: Former Computer Teacher Part 4 – Advice

Introduction:
Dear Reader,

At last, we get to the words of wisdom section.

This isn't just teaching advice. There are excellent little lessons about being a student—and a parent—in here.

~Ann

What advice do you have for new teachers?
Former Computer Teacher:
- Aim to be prepared for each lesson.
- Greet the students when they enter.
- Have something for them to do right away. Discipline problems happen when there is down time.

- Have high, but realistic expectations for the students and let them know that you expect them to be able to accomplish them.
- Reward hard work, but not too much. After all, it's what they are expected to do.

I once knew a teacher who maintained that you should never thank students for obeying the rules as if they did you a favor.

I'm not sure I totally agree with that, but I understand the spirit of it. I rather try to acknowledge good work/behavior as a motivation for others who are watching.

- Don't try to be the students' friend.
- Don't talk with them on social media.
- Don't talk down to the students.
- Treat them like you would like to be treated.
- Be there often to support them in their extracurricular activities.
- Notice something positive and good and acknowledge it in front of others.
- Short, heartfelt comments are more appreciated than lectures.
- Let them know the rules that you will enforce and then be consistent.
- Enforce the school rules even if you don't agree with them.

At my former school there was a published dress code, which I was not good at following, but I applaud my colleagues who were champs in this area. I felt there were too many loopholes to worry about, but I tried.

One time, after requiring my eighth graders to remove their jackets during class—we travel between buildings at our school, so coats do not remain in the lockers—I had the guidance counselor call me to the door and let me know that one of the students was allowed to keep her jacket on.

It seems that she had used her watch to text her mother—another violation—who called the school and requested that she be allowed to wear her coat.

There was a lot of smirking that day, but the lesson went on.

Me: That would annoy the heck out of me. The students would probably not have had a great day after that because it would be abundantly clear that stupid power plays are a very bad idea.

What do you think kids need to succeed at school?
- Every child needs educators who care if they succeed and who regularly assess and modify their own teaching styles to accommodate the students in their classroom.
- They need teachers who communicate with the administration and parents to try to nip problems in the bud and provide support to the extent that they are able.
- As a Christian school teacher, I would add that students need teachers who pray for their lives and needs.
- Every child needs to be treated and respected as an individual with talents and ideas.
- A child needs to feel he has something to offer to the school community.
- A child does not need to be coddled, but inspired, not by telling, but by the power of examples in life, stories, and great literature.
- Children need to know that there are ethical and moral principles that guide them to honorable acts and away from repugnant behavior.
- Curriculum and faculty matter.
- A child needs a safe environment and healthy habits at home and pride in their school in order to concentrate most fully at the job of being a student.

- Consistent and dependable rules and routines provide a hedge of protection for a child.
- Parents and teachers need to be advocates for the best interest of the child even if that at times requires discipline and pain.
- Children need to develop competence, at various levels and according to innate ability in the classical areas of math, science, history (and civics), and literature as well as exposure to foreign language, music, art, and physical education.

How did the pandemic affect teaching?

I only taught for three months during the pandemic having already planned to retire at the end of the year.

Since our original expectations were for schools to be closed for only a couple weeks, I found that teachers did not immediately kick into remote instruction, but instead gave written assignments. Some of us learned to make videos and so forth and holding a class on zoom was like watching a rerun of the Brady Bunch.

My experience with remote learning came primarily as I sat with my special needs (autistic) grandson as he was taught via zoom for the first semester of the 2020-2021 school year.

My impressions were that his third-grade teachers were working very hard to keep the class moving forward.

They were prepared with digital resources and provided direct instruction with all the specials, including music, technology, art, and physical education.

However, although my grandson sat quietly in front of his laptop (which the district provided) he seemed to miss most of what was happening even with an adult sitting with him the entire time directing his attention back to the screen.

His aide met him in breakout rooms regularly, but she often provided him answers when he hesitated, rather than waiting for him to work through the assignments in his own time.

What do you think he missed?
- the personal interaction with the teacher
- the chance to take a break when he needed it
- the learning that comes from watching the other students
- the social cues learned at the lunchroom table and on the playground

He has been dealing with the effects of those deficiencies in fourth grade.

I think the self-motivated students who relish independence from the physical classroom as a way of completing work quickly and gaining extra free time excelled with remote learning.

I wonder very seriously about many others.

Me: Thank you for taking the time to answer all of my nosy questions.

Takeaways:
- Teachers need to be adaptable.
- Kids need structure.
- Schools adapted for the pandemic, but many students still require personal interaction to succeed.

Chapter 10:
Episode 70: General Opinion:
Molehills to Die On
(Self-Advocacy vs. Stupid Defiance)

Introduction:

Dear Readers,

Let's focus on something the recent guests have brought up in a roundabout way. There's a huge difference between self-advocation and stupid defiance.

In Chapter 65, Brave Former Student said she didn't have the words to express her depression and other mental health struggles. She couldn't articulate that the lack of motivation had mental health and not laziness origins. If she had been able to find the words, she would have been able to advocate better with her teachers.

In Chapter 69, Former Computer Teacher spoke about the kid who used her watch to get her mom to call the school and demand an exception to the dress code rule about jackets. This is just one example of a silly thing to take a stand on.

One of my friends calls them molehills to die on. It's an apt description. I'll start with some basic definitions then move to some stories with my comments.

~Ann

Basic definitions:
What is a molehill to die on?
It's a relatively small issue someone has a strong opinion on and is willing to defend past the point of normal reason.

What is self-advocacy?
It's a skill that involves presenting one's point of view and needs in the hopes of gaining some concession (extension) or boon (favor).

What is stupid defiance?
It's when a student chooses a molehill to die on.

Disclaimer: Some examples are fictional recreations (meaning I filled in some details), but all are based on things that have happened.

Note: The examples will focus on stupid defiance. If self-advocacy had kicked in, the students in these scenarios would have made their point then dropped the issue.

Second note: All lines are paraphrased.

Scenario 1: (Improper use of chair)
Scene 1: A kid in the media center leaned back so that two chair legs were off the ground. A custodian asked the kid to put the chair down on all four legs.

Kid's Response: "You can't tell me what to do."

Scene 1 continued: A teacher asked the kid to put the chair down on all four legs.

Kid's Response: "No hablo inglés."

Side note: The kid is Latino.

Scene 1 continued again: The teacher flagged down an administrator to talk to the kid. At that point, the kid was removed from the media center, so the consequences are unknown.

My response to scenario 1:
The molehill: the issue of sitting in the chair properly

What made it worse: kid's defiance and sass

Analysis: The kid was downright rude to the custodian and the teacher. Both would have been remiss in their duty of care to let the kid continue to use the chair improperly. That's a stuffy way of saying, it's likely the chair would have fallen over and resulted in the kid cracking his head on a bookshelf.

Scenario 2: (Snapping fingers to get someone's attention)
Scene 2: A kid snapped his fingers to get his teacher's attention.

Teacher's response: "Don't you ever do that again. Do you have any idea how rude that is?"

Scene 2 continued: The kid seemed genuinely surprised to learn that snapping his fingers is not an appropriate way to get somebody's attention.

My response to scenario 2:
I view this scene as self-advocacy on the teacher's part. She saw something that was inappropriate and promptly informed the kid what exactly was wrong and why.

Scenario 3: (A joke gone horribly wrong followed by strong doses of sass and defiance)
Scene 3: Students were participating in a project to observe

decomposition. This involved actual dead rats. A young man touched the dead rat with a stick then made one of the girls think she'd accidentally touched the rat-contaminated side of that same stick. (I believe he had switched them out, but that's beside the point.)

The girl broke down and bawled.

The boy kept pressing the point by pretending to be grossed out by the thought of the girl touching him with rat-contaminated hands.

Teacher's response: "We don't play games with people's mental health. If anybody pulls a stunt like this again, I will fail you on the project."

Scene 3 continued: As the teacher delivered the warning, the one kid it was aimed at the most started talking to a friend.

Teacher: "You should really pay attention to what I'm saying."

Kid: "I was in the middle of a conversation."

Scene 3 continued again: The teacher started going over some notes with the students. The same student was on his phone.

Teacher: "Put your phone down."

Kid: "I am in the middle of something."

Teacher: "If you can't listen to me, you will have to visit the vice principal."

Kid: "I would love to."

Scene 3 moves forward again: The teacher sends the student to the central office. The kid doesn't move.

Teacher: "Now."

Kid: "I'll go in a few minutes."

Teacher: "Would you like me to escort you?"

Kid: "I would feel so much safer."

Scene 3 moves forward yet again: The teacher called somebody from hall duty to watch her class while she took the student down to the office. As they were walking there the student stopped to talk to a friend.

Teacher: "Keep walking."

Kid: "You know it's really rude to interrupt someone talking."

Scene 3 cherry on top: The student earns himself a detention. He then asked the vice principal for a phone charger.

Kid's side of the story: The rat thing was taken out of context. Things just escalated.

My response to scenario 3:
Reading the transcript of that is like watching a car wreck happen in slow motion.

The initial joke was in poor taste, but these things happen with kids. Not everyone has the same sense of humor.

Where it went wrong was the boy continuing to press the point, ignoring the teacher's admonishment about inappropriate lab behavior, and his continued sass.

Sass can be amusing in very small doses, but like a spice, too much can ruin everything.

If the kid had dropped the ill-fated joke immediately, things would have been fine. The class may have still gotten the don't-mess-with-people's-mental-health lecture, but that's about it.

Even if the student hadn't been paying attention but pretended to toe the line when called out, things would have been fine.

There are about four places here where the student saw a line in the sand and deliberately stepped over it.

In those cases, the teacher has to follow through with discipline if she wants to maintain order in the classroom.

Takeaways:
- Explaining your side is good but thinking you can never do wrong is bad.
- The initial offense usually isn't the main issue. The problem kicks in when the student digs-in and defends that molehill.
- Students usually get several warnings, but they generally wait to get yelled at before they choose to follow the rule.
- Jokes can go wrong. Apologize and move on.

Chapter 11:
Episode 71 – General Opinion: Trust Issues – Written (and Unwritten) Absence Rules

Introduction:

Dear Reader,

As you might have guessed, I like writing.

What you may not have known is that I plan to attend a large writing conference in a few months.

The problem is that it's a week long and right in between a few breaks.

Most schools have an unwritten rule about faculty not taking off days that are right up against holidays/ days the district is closed. Some have even gone so far as to put it in writing that you need their blessing—and extenuating circumstances—to do it.

Let's chat about trust issues.

~Ann

Rhymes, reasons, rationale:

While I complained to a friend, she made a great point. I already knew it, but it's always nicer when somebody spells it out for you. I was making the point that very few other professions distrust their people to the point that they dictate when and how personal days can be used.

My friend noted that teaching is a profession where you are responsible for others, so it makes sense that they (districts) wouldn't want everybody taking off the same days.

With the way things are right now, substitute teachers are in short supply.

Side note: Hat's off to substitute teachers. That is not an easy job. Bottom line is you need enough teachers or people willing to step in so your school can function.

That's the reason such written and unwritten rules about absences exist.

I get it. I just don't like it.

My mini-saga:

Yesterday, I talked to my immediate boss and the school principal. Each said okay, then promptly kicked it up the chain of command. The principal also said to contact the head of human resources and the superintendent.

I did so.

Got an email back from the superintendent that the HR person would email me.

I thanked her.

Reminder: I work in a place with a very oddball rotating schedule, so it's anybody's guess about who has off what period what days.

Today, on one of my periods off, I went to the administration office to see about scheduling that meeting because these things are usually way less complicated in person.

Before then, never laid eyes on this woman.

Conversation went something like this:

Me: *Explains purpose of visit.

HR lady: "I'm in the middle of something. I will get back to you by email. Then, we can go through it the way it's normally done ... by email."

I thanked her and left.

As of 8:00 p.m., there's still no email from her. One of my friends pointed out that a board meeting is coming up, so she may be running around like crazy for that.

That's understandable, but the dismissive attitude was still interesting and not very impressive for somebody whose entire job is dealing with people.

I'm aware that not everybody checks emails at all hours of the day, but how long does it take to send a we-should-schedule-a-meeting email?

Guess the saga has no conclusion thus far ... that's disappointing.

Tragic backstory:

Once upon a time, a naïve younger, very untenured version of me signed up for a cool conference in Hawaii.

She then played the good egg and went to inform the school and got denied.

Union people said: Wait until you're tenured, then don't tell them, just do it.

Good plan, but the folks raised me to be honest.

It shouldn't be this difficult to take personal days.
In almost every other profession, you get two weeks off to use as you will. One of my friends who doesn't work in a school said her job has unlimited paid time off. That's an interesting concept. She said it's mostly helpful to the company because they're not responsible for paying out accumulated paid time off when people retire.

Random answer to reflex rebuttal that most non-teachers have:
Summer doesn't count. Although our health insurance will carry over, unless we've scheduled your paychecks to stretch through the summer, we're not paid for those ten weeks.

Back on track:
Once people make it to the working world, many are workaholics. Getting them to take a day off can be difficult.

Teachers tend not to take frivolous days off because it's devilishly difficult to plan such things.

A writing conference isn't frivolous anyway, but it's also not my content area, so there's no "educational" benefit. Translation: There's no seeming benefit to the school.

Side note: I'm hearing other people are taking high school kids to the conference. Don't think I'd ever be that nuts, but more power to them. (Day trips are stressful walkathons where I end up counting and recounting heads all day.) It will be an excellent experience for the young writers.

Why is honest the harder road?
I suppose that's a philosophical question. There are underhanded ways to do this. I could schedule three personal days in the middle

of the week and call-in sick Monday and Friday.

What's likely to happen?
I'm tenured now, so I'll likely do it anyway.
They may dock my pay. Will have to keep you posted on that front because it seems the situation is set to move at the speed of a glacier here.

The wrong message:
Whether intentional or not, situations like this are annoying because they are channeling some not-so-great messages.

What messages?
- We don't trust you.
- Be dishonest. It's easier.
- Your heart and soul belongs to the school.
- You can take your personal days, if we deem it so.

Takeaways:
- Policies exist to prevent system abuse. That's fine. But making everything an epic fight isn't exactly a morale booster.
- Schools need to show that they trust their people.

Chapter 12:
Episode 72 – General Opinion: Teacher Appreciation Week (Also Known as Carb Week)

Introduction:

Dear Reader,

I've never been a huge fan of appreciation weeks. Maybe that's just the cynic in me.

I'm the sort that feels Valentine's Day, Mother's Day, and Father's Day are kind of lame, money grubbing holidays endorsed by card and candy makers.

On the flip side, it is good to set aside time to appreciate something or someone because people tend to take loved ones for granted.

Don't get me started on National this-and-that days and month celebrations.

I do always enjoy the breakfast, luncheon, and bagel-a-thons that happen during the week.

In a perfect world, people wouldn't feel underappreciated in their jobs.

~Ann

How did Teacher's Appreciation Week go?
Bagels. So many bagels.

I find it amusing and interesting that something as simple as a bagel can be very different. I think we had bagels three times during Teacher Appreciation Week.

The first instance, they were soft and large. The second time, they were dense and hard but had a variety of very different cream cheese spreads. The third time, they were large and normal level firm.

Yummy lunch:
The parents always put on a very nice catered breakfast/luncheon that runs most of the day. I'm sure it's a tremendous amount of work that costs a lot.

Personal level:
I got a nice small gift from one of my students. I don't think it cost them much, but the effort was a nice gesture.

Side musing:
At the high school level, teacher gifts are rare. I believe that's because there are a lot more teachers in normal high school and middle school models.

In elementary school, the main teacher is responsible for all core subjects and the class travels or has a few special programs teachers visit them on a set schedule.

What should you get teachers if you want to give 'em stuff?
- Gift cards. – Most people don't know teachers well enough to predict allergies, likes, and dislikes of consumable stuff.

- School supplies you know the teacher uses. High quality pencils have a way of walking off every class period. Eraser caps usually get consumed by the students at frightening rates too.
- If a teacher uses stickers, grab some fun stickers. If they hoard Post-it notes, grab a pack or two.
- Thoughtful notes and simple thank you emails can go a long way.

Unrealistic wish item:
An honesty card – lets you tell one parent exactly what you think of their kid's paltry efforts in your class.

Stuff is nice but thought matters too.

One of my friends got a hand-written letter from a student. I think it basically said she wished she could afford to buy something for the teacher, included a thanks for being awesome type message, and a little doodle of some sort.

Not sure if my friend kept the letter, but I do know she cherished it.

Unless you know someone well, a physical gift is likely going to be just another thing cluttering the desk.

I read a random article put out by www.forbes.com that mentioned things like plants, candles, and tea kettles. I know mugs is a common one.

Things to consider:
- Plants require care.
- Candles come in a gazillion scents. Some people are allergic to certain scents. Even if one doesn't have an allergy to strong candle scents, it's likely the person has 2-3 they're fond of out of the 20-30 options out there. It may

be difficult getting something they would enjoy.

- If somebody likes tea, they probably already have a kettle. Some places in a school aren't technically supposed to have appliances. (Something about fire hazards.)
- People get particular about their mugs. Like a tea kettle, those who use mugs likely have a few dozen favorites. I'm not saying you can't add one more. I'm saying that if you give somebody a mug, it's likely going to be one among many.

In the perfect world ...
There wouldn't be a need for special appreciation weeks. Everybody would feel that their efforts are appreciated.

Things students can do to show they appreciate the hard work involved in teaching:
A lot of these are going to sound obvious, but sometimes, it's good to state things simply.

- Engage with the lesson. It's hard to learn passively anyway.
- Laugh at the lame jokes.
- Make eye contact.
- Smile on occasion. If storybook characters can smile eight times in the span of a novel, you can smile four times in a school year.
- Observe and obey the stuffy rules about phone usage. Phones are awesome, but it's not a great feeling to be talking to someone who's ignoring you.

Takeaways:
- Stuff is okay, but you don't need stuff to convey appreciation.
- Students can show appreciation in small but powerful ways like engaging with a lesson.
- If you don't know somebody that well, gift cards make better gifts than very specific items.

Chapter 13:
Episode 72 – Special Guest: Former Teacher with Friends Beyond the Classroom

Introduction:

Dear Reader,

This next guest did a very quick, informal interview with me via one of the social media platforms. She touches upon a few points that I'd love to expand on.

I haven't pinned down what exactly she taught, but from her answers, I'd guess some sort of elementary school.

~Ann

Note: I'm going to go with Former Teacher with Friends as her title because the full thing is a wee bit long.

What was your favorite part of teaching?

Former Teacher with Friends: I loved watching the kids' faces light up when they realized you can connect letters to make words.

My response: The ah-ha moment is a triumph for everybody. It's always delightful to witness and can be about any lesson really. I recently had the pleasure of witnessing a baby take her first unassisted steps. That look of accomplishment is priceless.

How about the least favorite part of teaching?

Former Teacher with Friends: What I liked least was that parents didn't keep up with the students at home (reinforce learning) and they fell behind during long breaks.

My response: The importance of parental involvement cannot be overstated. I'm not sure I've devoted a whole chapter to that point, but I'll certainly have to do so soon.

Teachers only get kids part of the time. Elementary teachers might get them a few hours a day. High school teachers get them 45 minutes every day to about 2 hours every few days, depending on the schedule.

Kids never stop learning.

Observation is one of the most powerful means of absorbing information. Attitudes and actions also speak volumes. So, when the parents help reinforce lessons at home, kids have a much easier time mastering topics.

What do you do now?

Former Teacher with Friends: I'm a writer, though I initially left teaching to move to L.A. to work on movie sets, help organize beach clean-ups, and work for Disney and Universal.

My response: That's awesome. Are movie sets as glamorous as our imaginations usually paint them out to be? By the way, I've read some of your recent works, and they're a lot of fun.

Do you stay in touch with any former students?

Former Teacher with Friends: Yes. I'm friends with many former students and their families on social media, and many told me they enjoyed learning about science with me, especially space and marine biology.

My response: I texted one of my former students before sitting down to write this, and I'm also in touch with at least one of my former teachers.

Teachers will interact with dozens of students throughout their careers. Most move on from your class and never look back. But there are usually a few who check in from time to time for one reason or another. It's always intriguing to see them grow up.

Do you remember anything about being a student? What is one of your toughest memories from that time?

Former Teacher with Friends: One of my worst memories as a student was when I couldn't afford to buy the supplies needed to make a pinata, and I was given detention for showing up unprepared.

However, the other students told me they would have given me what I needed if they knew. That flipped it to a good memory.

My response: Kids can be cruel, but it's little stories like these that remind me there are wonderful ones too. It's interesting how perspective can flip a memory good or bad.

I'm not even sure we're allowed to require students to bring in supplies for just this reason. (The fact that some students may not be able to afford the supplies.)

It's always a best practice to provide the basics for any project. I let my students bring their own supplies as they like or use mine.

What's one of your fondest memories from your own schooling career?

Former Teacher with Friends: As a student, one of my favorite memories was a teacher who gave us five sour cherry candies if we aced a test.

Everyone helped each other and most of the class did very well. We shared with the ones that didn't but tried.

My response: I try to avoid feeding the children, but Dum Dums (small lollipops made in a factory that's low on allergens) are usually a hit.

Takeaways:
- Kindness and candy go a long way.
- Parental support and interest in the child's learning experiences are both vital.
- Not being able to afford stuff puts some kids in a very awkward position.

Chapter 14:
Episode 74 – Hall Duty Diaries: The Cream Puff Generation

Introduction:
Dear Ann,

I've been a teacher for a while now.

I don't have a set story for you, just some observations.

In my humble opinion, we're raising a generation of cream puffs. (Looks good on the outside, but squishes in all directions at the slightest pressure.)

Here are my observations in no particular order:
1. Kids are choosing to fail. – The academic support teacher does way more work than the kids he's trying to support. I always see him running around asking kids for missing assignments.
2. One of my students will do the harder assignments and just not hand in the easy stuff.
3. I overheard some of my students talking about summer school. The one kid didn't care that he'd fail because his

mom just did his summer school assignments for him. (It costs a few hundred dollars, but the kids aren't paying for it, so they don't care.)

4. Some students are cream puffs. A girl rushed off to the restroom in tears because she had to participate in a forensic science project involving a dead rat.

5. I've been in a few IEP meetings for one girl. The mother has her convinced she's "just no good" at math, but really, the kid is capable.

6. My colleague and I just received a transfer student from another school. He's coming in with almost all failing grades. We were informed that he's supposed to just audit the class for the rest of the year. That's a terrible idea!

7. One of my kids had a freakout over a broken pen leaking ink on him. The boy's mother wonders why he doesn't have any friends, but I've seen his behavior in class. He's just not nice to the other students.

8. One of my friends works in a special needs room. She has to call a girl every morning to cajole her into coming into school. The parents have lost all control. My friend told me that every single one of the 8 kids she has is there because of poor parenting.

   The school (teachers, counselors, special services people) spend a lot of time and effort coming up with a plan for each child and often, the parents stick with it for a day or two, then drop the ball on the plan.

9. A friend once had guidance come to her and say that a kid wanted to take forensics but couldn't do CSI type shows. The question was could the curriculum be modified to let her take the course without anything suspenseful or that would otherwise make the child uncomfortable. Answer: Uh, no.

How did we get here? How do we get back to creating responsible adults?

~ A Teacher on Hall Duty

My response:
Those are some intriguing mini-tales and some very difficult questions you raise.

Side note: I'm never looking at a cream puff the same way again. That's an interesting analogy.

Musings on how we got here and why we stay here: (Here being a place where students are okay with floating along failing.)
The lack of true failure issue often ties back to money. School funding is linked to *success*. Success can be fudged based on where you set the bar.

One of the toughest parts of teaching is watching a kid struggle. There's an innate tendency to want to just do the task for them.

It's not much of a stretch to believe that parents often have the same problems. Teenagers are surly creatures. About the quickest way to get them to bite your head off is greet them when they get home. I can imagine questioning them about missing work or class behavior goes over as smoothly as sandpaper.

Motivation can be tricky. Many kids are internally motivated or really like getting A's. But there's a delicate balance. Once kids get it stuck in their heads that they can't do something or just aren't good at something motivation crashes and burns to ashes.

Schools were never meant to take on parental roles, but more and more, some of the un-fun parts of parenting are being forced upon schools. It's a short-term, short-sighted solution that will have mediocre results at best in most cases.

This generation has the added burden of social media to bear.

Musings on what needs to change to fix the broken sections:

Breaking through the mental barriers kids erect can be difficult. Part of the battle involves defeating the self-doubt they cling to like a favorite teddy bear. In the short term, breaking a task down to the point where the student can find immediate gratification sort of success can help. Work up to the longer, harder stuff.

What you do will largely depend on how much spare energy you have as a teacher. If you're already treading water, I guess just keep on treading. If you have the mental margin to tackle some of the issues, try to connect with your students and teach them those unwritten life lessons.

To enact the biggest change, you likely have to tackle the huge issues like how funding gets distributed. Like anything political, the waters turn murky very quickly.

Kids don't always realize how much they need structure, order, and discipline. To the best of your abilities, establish these things in your miniature classroom kingdom.

Kids don't need the adults around them to be their friends. They need authority figures who they can respect and feel respected by. You can only fix the parenting side of the equation with your own kids.

Teach kids how to be responsible about their social media presences. (Most previous generations admit to doing dumb things. There just wasn't a camera in their face preserving the moment.)

Pithy truths:

Let's get back to the basics.

Teachers, change what you can. Don't sweat the rest.

Parents, teachers, and schools in general want what's best for the students.

When conflict arises, attempt to de-escalate the situation. Focus more on solutions, less on blame.

Takeaways:

Unfortunately, there's no magic bullet that will fix school problems.

Teaching is an important job, but it's only one portion of your life. Pour what energy you can into doing it well, but also, enact world-changing one person at a time rather than lamenting what cannot be changed overnight.

Chapter 15:
Episode 75 – Special Guest: Part-Time Student (Public School)

Introduction:

Dear Reader,

Tracking down students willing to talk about their experiences can be tricky, but I'm happy to say I found one who can represent the public-school experience.

Part of the vision for this project is to represent all perspectives as evenly as possible.

I think the only type of person harder to find than students is administrators. I'll work on that.

~Ann

What was your schooling situation?

Part-Time Student: I grew up going to public schools for all grades. I graduated from high school three years ago.

After graduation, I took a two-year break, and now, I am focusing on online school for college.

The idea is to eventually make it to an on-campus school at a university.

How big was your high school?
Part-Time Student: I had pretty big schools. My graduating class alone was around 600 people.

Me: I worked at a school that had about that many. The graduation ceremony was long, but I guess they had a lot of experience with the large number. They had two people reading and whipped through those names like nobody's business.

Can you describe a typical day of high school?
Part-Time Student: A typical day in any of my schools was of course multiple subjects, mixed with general education classes and classes that helped build upon creativity, hobbies, and exploration of various activities. Of course, you can't forget the much-needed breaks.

Me: Breaks are much appreciated.

I do not envy students.

They have a tough job.

Even getting used to 6-ish different people's quirks and ways of doing things can be challenging.

What was the best and worst part of school?
Part-Time Student: The best part of school was definitely the people. Friends, classmates, teachers who cared, campus employees who took the time to get to know you.

The worst part, of course, was the actual work, especially when it didn't seem to have much of a purpose. Some projects and homework were enjoyable and helped grow the brain. The rest of it—not so much.

Me: Relevancy can be an issue.

I do often get asked, "When am I ever going to use this?" (I also get asked what I ate for breakfast, so don't think the question too profound. Usually, it's a time-honored distraction tactic.)

The full answer is, of course, "That depends on your life choices." But I tend to give a very short speech about it training them to think, problem solve, work through things, and manage their time.

Did you have a favorite subject?
Part-Time Student: Favorite subjects changed by year, depending on teachers and the activities they gave to us.

English was always one of my easier subjects, and I enjoyed most of the science classes.

Music was always the best, as it is my passion.

Me: I liked science, and I'm forever grateful to my 8th grade and elementary teachers for laying out the grammar rules for writing.

How did you get your socializing in?
Part-Time Student: Socializing was easy, especially because I attended schools with lots of students.

When I was younger, I was a lot shier around people I didn't know, but as I got older, I forced myself to get out there more.

I was able to make friends in classes, clubs, the tennis team, and even at events.

Me: That's a great list of places to find people you connect with.

What advice do you have for students who might be new to the public school system?
Part-Time Student: This is where you start figuring out who you are.

There will be TONS of influences, both good and bad.

I would say, make it worth it. Do what your heart says (with some logic too, of course), get out there, and forget about what people may think about you.

People are going to be people, so why not be you?

Me: Excellent advice. I especially like the part where you acknowledge that there are good and bad influences available in your school.

What worked out well for you?
Part-Time Student: I did pretty well in school, and I did well on the tennis team too.

I would say all my years of schooling helped build me to who I am today.

What did you struggle with?
Part-Time Student: I definitely struggled with math, as it was not my friend.

I also struggled with friendships at some point. I felt alone until I found new friends. These are people who I'm still in contact with every day.

Me: Yeah, I hear you. Math and I stopped agreeing around 8th grade.

Finding the right friend group can be hard. I see how my students treat each other, and sometimes, I'm just like "get better friends."

Would you have done anything different if you could?

Part-Time Student: I'm pretty happy with how things turned out. I feel that I definitely had to focus on my academic schooling, but I was also able to enjoy the experience for the most part and have fun.

Some of my friends focused just on school, and would never go out, and they'd be working so hard to get everything ready to go straight to college.

There's nothing wrong with preparation, but I took a two-year break after high school to serve at a church mission. Now, I'm back in school, I have a really great job, and I'm happily dating someone.

Everyone's story will be different, and you don't need to follow the same set path that everyone else may go on. Make it yours!

Me: Don't think I have to add much to that.

Takeaways (straight from our brave guest):

- There will be things in school that seem pointless, but many of the lessons do actually carry over down the line.
- You have the chance to meet lifelong friends.
- Public schools (all schools really) have a ton of influences, both good and bad.
- People emphasize getting to college immediately, but it's possible to take a break, do something you love that gives you life experience, and then, return for another round of formal education. (There are also solid careers that do not require more "formal education.")
- Classes, clubs, sports teams, and events are some of the many places where you can connect with people while at school.

Chapter 16:
Episode 76 – Special Guest: Sassy Substitute's Year End Thoughts

Introduction:

Dear Reader,

High schools around the United States are wrapping up in the middle of May.

The following thoughts were first shared on a social media post from Sassy Substitute. (She was previously featured in Chapter 33 and Chapter 39.)

Substitute teaching is a different beast than regular teaching. That just means it has unique challenges and experiences to weed through.

Thankfully, there are people like Sassy Substitute willing to step in when the regular teachers need to step away for one reason or another.

~Ann

Sassy Substitute's Year-End Thoughts:
Sassy Substitute: Thus ends my 2021-2022 school year of subbing.

Thought 1: It's been ... interesting.

Thought 2: I've learned so many things.

Me: Kids, regardless of age, do have many lessons to teach us.

Sassy Substitute thought 3: I even considered becoming a teacher for five seconds then realized I am better as a come-at-the-last-second-and-wing-it kinda gal who never has to grade homework or deal with the long-term stuff.

Me: I'm curious how your perspective would change if you were a regular classroom teacher, but then, the world would lose an excellent substitute teacher.

In many ways, being a substitute teacher is more difficult. It's hard to make connections when you're in a classroom daily, let alone once every so often as needed.

Sassy Substitute thought 4: Teachers are honestly some of the strongest people, emotionally and physically.

Me: It's a surprisingly demanding job. Every new school year, I need to regain my *school legs*.

Side note: I find climbing lab counters kind of fun, but I fear the day when my knees balk at that idea.

Sassy Substitute thought 5: If you're wondering, yes, I plan to sub next school year.

I enjoy the kids, and I already drive there anyway. So, why not? Plus, I get lots of fun material to share.

Me: Excellent. I would personally miss seeing your hilarious stories from the teaching front.

Sassy Substitute thought 6:

Before I sign off until August, a few things:

- If you have extra pencils, donate them to a teacher. Kids "forget" them daily.
- Some teachers need couches or comfy chairs in their classrooms for prep period lounging. (In case you are getting rid of any.)
- Lots of teachers need more storage. (In case you're getting rid of bookshelves.)
- Many teachers have mini-fridges and microwaves but not all. (In case you are getting rid of any.) They would literally be so happy to receive these!
- Email your kids' teachers and tell them what an awesome job they did. Most days are hard, and they will keep those happy words handy to boost their spirits.
- Teach your children to be respectful. I can never say this enough times. I can handle a class full of unruly kids until one of them disrespects me, then I'm just over it.
- Your kids are hilarious and goofy and sweet and annoying.

Until 2022-2023 ... This is Sassy Substitute, signing off for the summer.

My response:
That's a fantastic list of practical advice for parents and the general public.

I cannot tell you how many pencils I go through each day. It's less now that I stopped putting them out. I still have them, but the kids have to remember to ask for one and endure my what-the-heck-happened-to-yours question if they wish to claim one.

I personally wouldn't have the room for a comfy couch, but I will admit to napping in the prep room. Same for bookcases, microwaves, and refrigerators, but I can see those coming in handy in many schools.

The respect thing is absolutely vital. In the last few days, I've had to call kids on some of the ways they treat each other and my class time. They may pass some rude comments off as joking, but they still need to learn to be kinder to each other.

I try to instill in the students that there will be times they want something from a teacher, so they need to be cognizant of the reputation they build.

Teachers will do the best they can for students, but it's a whole heap easier to go out of your way for a kid you genuinely like and respect.

Respect can take multiple forms.

Quick overview of practical respect:

- Adhere to the class-specific rules about phones, food, talking, calling out answers, bathroom requests, etc.
- Ask instead of assuming anything.
- Come prepared to class – This includes having paper and a writing implement. If cost is a factor, certainly feel free to ask for the materials, but once given, be responsible enough to keep track of the pencil/ pen that's given to you.
- Address the teacher respectfully.
- Watch how you talk about other people (friends, other teachers, friends' parents).
- Curb your tendency to curse in an academic environment.
- Respond to requests the first time. Do not wait to be called out on something by name.
- Follow proper procedure when it comes to asking for an extension or some other favor.
- Treat peers with respect.

- Treat class time with respect. (I've seen kids steal each other's Airpods because it's funny. They returned it eventually, but this completely disrupted the learning environment for this kid because he spent the next 15 minutes interrogating them about it.)

Takeaways:
- Respect cannot be over-emphasized. It starts at home. Teenagers can be moody, but when they snap at you, correct the behavior. If they're only getting the instruction from school, it will be far less effective.
- Teach kids to be responsible about their school supplies.
- A kind word goes a long way.

Chapter 17:
Episode 77 – General Opinion: Effort Snitches (and Other Euphemisms)

Introduction:
Dear Reader,

Whether you believe testing is the way to go or not, the truth remains that formally assessing students through paper-based, question-and-answer style tests remains the primary means of measuring student success.

I recently had a discussion with some other teachers in a social media group about what we call such entities.

Though I could not tell you whether the tendency to turn to a kinder term is a recent trend or something that's been around for years, apparently, many people use some sort of euphemism instead of calling a formal assessment a test or a quiz.

I haven't seen hard data one way or another, but if there's psychological comfort in avoiding a particular word, I suppose it can't hurt.

~Ann

What do you call tests and other formal assessments? Some people go with the obvious answer:

I believe one person even said they just call tests what they are.

- Tests – This one got a few votes.
- Quests – I've used this before. It's something in between a quiz and a test in terms of weight.
- Quizzes – generally accepted to be worth less than a test
- Assessments
- Annoying things – I don't think this person was serious, but I had to include it anyway because it made me laugh.
- Content based assessments – This one's a little too formal for my tastes.
- Benchmarks – practice state tests
- A picture of what you already know and what I still need to teach – The proponent of this one admitted it's a tad clunky, but it works for her.

Random musing:

Maybe by the time I get to formally assessing the students, my creativity is all tapped out. Or maybe my literal tendencies are just showing. Whatever the reason, I generally stick with calling tests and quizzes by their given names.

Use a euphemism:

- Boss
- Game Day
- Opportunities
- Celebrations of Knowledge
- Show What You Know – got a few votes

Arbitrary favorite euphemism award:

My favorite euphemism is Show What You Know. One of my colleagues uses this one.

She teaches the advanced levels of the subject (honors and

Advanced Placement). Her students tend to get freaked out by formal assessments. Using a euphemism takes some of the sting out of the concept, I guess.

If it works for her, I'm all for it.

My students think we have a test or quiz every day. (Maybe every week, but even then, they'll vary in weight and design.) We might even have two in a week, mostly if they're different purposes, such as a memorization quiz and a more math-based quiz.

A quiz really is a lower-stakes instance of showing me what they know, so the title fits. Thus far, I just can't bring myself to call them that. It's late enough in the year that any change would just get me a strange look from the students. Perhaps, I'll give it a go next year.

Discussion of Runner-ups:
Boss and Game Day require a little more explanation and build up to get the kids to buy into the analogy they represent.

Boss:
One of my friends uses the term Boss for his tests, but that's because he works the entire class into a sort of role-playing game. He also has the drawing chops to make up a cartoon sketch to represent each boss that needs to be defeated.

This gets high marks for creativity but low marks for transferability. Translation: I don't think the term Boss will work for most people unless they are willing to create an entire game around it.

Game Day:
If you'd like to use this one, you should probably at least explain the sports analogy. As you do various activities that tie-in to the topic, frame it as practice. Then, Game Day for a wrap-up assessment makes sense.

Opportunities:
This is almost as straightforward as calling a test a test, but I suppose it's a tad more friendly.

Celebrations of Knowledge:
I can almost guarantee high schoolers will respond with a long-suffering look or an eyeroll. I do like the optimism inherent to the phrase.

My favorite responses come from the elementary school teachers:
- Effort Snitch
- Check ins – second grade
- Attention Span Tattle Tales
- Show Me Your Skills Page
- A Job You Do By Yourself – Kindergarten
- Valid data to help me make decisions on how to support and challenge you

Arbitrary favorite elementary euphemism award:
It was very close between Attention Span Tattle Tale and Effort Snitch, but I have to go with Effort Snitch because it's snappier. They are essentially saying the same thing.

The test is something that measures how well the student has mastered the concept. Typically, that's going to correlate very closely to how much effort has been put into accomplishing that goal.

Takeaways:
- Some people (okay, it's me, I'm some people) get their straightforward button stuck on the on setting and call formal assessments tests and quizzes.
- Others get creative or tie it into a wider analogy such as sports or video games.

- Some get cute and creative, though I'm fairly certain Attention Span Tattle Tale only works in elementary school.

Chapter 18:
Episode 78 – Special Guest: Multi-Sport Coach Talks Shop

Introduction:

Dear Reader,

I'm not quite to off-my-lawn level, but somedays, I feel like I'm getting there.

I finally got to have a semi-formal, sit-down chat with a guy who coaches the bowling team and the junior varsity girls' lacrosse team.

Those are two very different sports. Also, I found his insights into junior varsity vs. varsity interesting (and informative).

~Ann

Facts about high school bowling:
- It's a winter sport that lasts about two and a half months
- It has a wider pool of kids who will turn out for tryouts.
- It requires more skill, less raw athleticism.

- People coming into the program do not have to have any prior experience. Everybody can improve with practice.
- The program tends to be smaller than some of the other teams.
- Practices are often run on different days because there are only so many lanes available.
- Practices of JV (junior varsity) and varsity happen side by side due to the nature of the sport

The coach's observations concerning bowling:

- You can definitely tell which of the bowlers plays other sports. Those who play other sports tend to come with a mental resilience that is lacking in those who only bowl.
- Usually don't have a problem getting the kids to show up for a practice.
- There tends to be less cliques than other sports, such as high school girls' lacrosse.

Facts about junior varsity high school girls' lacrosse:

- It's a spring sport that runs from early March to the middle/end of May.
- The point of a JV team is to be a feeder program for varsity, so commitment to practices doesn't usually affect game time. (Players will get some time in every game.)
- The entire program might have over thirty girls, but the JV team would be around 13 girls.
- Varsity players are allowed to play in JV games.

The coach's observations concerning girls' lacrosse:

- It was frustrating at times because some of my players had almost zero commitment to practice. I would get a dozen different excuses (family event, doctor's appointment, work commitment, forgot about practice) or not even get an excuse.

- The fact that I was expected to let them play in games meant there was no incentive for them to make that commitment to practice.
- Sometimes, I didn't even have enough kids to run certain drills.
- When kids don't practice together, they lack team cohesion. This is true for the kids who don't show up for practice and for the ones coming down from varsity. Varsity players practice with that team.
- I had a Junior on defense who wanted to play offense. She would get out of position, putting more pressure on her teammates to cover for the fact that the player she was supposed to cover is now wide open.

Even with the frustrations, would you do it again?

Multi-Sport Coach: Yes. It was overall an enjoyable experience. It's both interesting and challenging to work with a very wide spread of skills. Some of the girls had never picked up a lacrosse stick before the season, and others have been playing for many years.

There are a few leagues around, but the level of casual interest isn't there like it is with soccer or baseball or even basketball.

There are equipment limitations that prevent pickup games. For soccer or basketball, you need the right kind of ball, a handful of people, and some made up goals or a public park court.

Benefits of being a coach:

- You get to recognize and develop relationships with kids you don't have in class.
- You have some influence over kids who are on your team.

Changes over the years:

Multi-Sport Coach: There's been a mindset shift from the time when I played high school sports. When we lost big, the bus was silent or at least very subdued because most of the players stewed over the loss.

We'd spend time reflecting on what went wrong and what we needed to do to prevent that from happening again.

When my kids lose, they're laughing and blasting music two seconds later. I'm not sure if that's a good thing or a bad thing.

On the one hand, it's good they're not emotionally gutted by a loss. Conversely, it's also a huge sign they don't really care much about it, and that's a terrible attitude for fostering improvement.

My response:
Once upon a time, I coached middle school girls' soccer. It was an interesting experience but not one I'm eager to repeat.

I suppose it depends on what you want from and for your team. At the level I was working with, we got in a few wins, but we also certainly went up against teams that far outmatched us. I accepted this. So, I don't think there was much stewing going on during the bus rides home.

Not sure where I stand on the issue of stewing over losses.

I agree that it'd be nice if the kids took the sport more seriously, but in the grand scheme of life, their lacrosse skills probably aren't going to get them a college scholarship or future career playing the sport. So, being unfazed by devastating losses isn't necessarily a bad thing.

Takeaways:
- Mindset and commitment to the sport and the team are important.
- The JV level is meant to be a training ground, but it's hindered by some of the unspoken rules concerning playing time.

- It seems like kids brush off losses easier these days. The multi-sport coach and I have yet to decide of that's a good or a bad thing.

Chapter 19:
Episode 79 – Soapbox General Opinion: The (Literal) Price of Integrity

Introduction:

Dear Reader,

Sorry for the stuffy title.

This chapter is a continuation from Chapter 71 General Opinion: Trust Issues - Written (and Unwritten) Absence Rules.

I've been a teacher for a while now. If you've read some of my other opinions, you should know that I try to be fair and open-minded about even the silliest of school policies.

It's always a heck of a lot easier to be tolerant of silly school policies that don't bite you in the butt.

Brace yourselves, this could be a bit soapbox-y because I find the whole situation genuinely disturbing.

~Ann

Summary of the mini-saga to date:

- Inquired about missing a week in the upcoming school year. The chain went from my supervisor to the principal to the human resources person and the superintendent.
- The superintendent said the HR person would handle it.
- Took a week and about three separate emails to get the HR person to schedule a meeting. She never showed up to that one (it was via Google Meet).
- Played email tag and finally got a new meeting scheduled for Wednesday (the week after the saga started). She didn't show up. After waiting a half-hour, I called her and got a face-to-face meeting where I got to present my question and hear her answer.

My takeaways from the meeting with the Human Resources woman:

- Don't take Monday off or you won't be paid for the previous Thursday-Friday (which my district has off for state conferences).
- Take two personal days off. Take two unpaid days off.
- The HR woman read me part of the employee handbook. I don't even have an updated copy of that, but what she read me sounded like "more than three personal days in a row require superintendent approval." When pressed about this, she indicated that because it was a total of four days I would need off, it still falls under the *needs-approval* banner. (My point was why can't I take three personal days and one unpaid day off?)
- I'm going to have to speak with my union people about this because the handbook wording is purposefully vague.

Brief informal conversation with union building representative:

People have handled this two ways:

- Above board – seek superintendent approval and lay all your cards on the table. Such leaves are usually granted for extenuating circumstances.
- Below board – file for some personal days, then file for some sick days. (Even if they require a doctor's note, those are pretty easy to come by.)

Reflections, rhetorical questions, and rantings (maybe some raving):

Some of my frustration with the situation stems from it taking a solid week to get a meeting with the head of Human Resources.

I understand she's a very busy person and that she has a lot of individual fires that need addressing, which could push my next-year concern to the back burner. However, the amount of chasing I did seems excessive.

What she quoted to me was essentially the worst-case scenario.

Can I afford to be docked two days?

Me: *grumbles* Yeah, but it still stinks.

Friend incensed on my behalf: You shouldn't have to be docked.

Me (responding to incensed friend): Agreed, but logic and schools aren't always compatible.

Recap of the policies I'm running up against:

- One cannot take off the day after holidays (any day the district is closed during the regular school term)
- One cannot take off more than three personal days without the superintendent's approval.

Reasons why the policies exist:

- Schools need enough teachers to run. Having everybody file for days off near holidays would be bad for staffing concerns.

- Not certain about the reasoning for the second point. We are given five personal days (one of the most generous of any school I've worked for, but I am not certain on the logic of it having to be spread out).

Note: The only reasoning that made a little sense was one of my friends telling me it's a control thing.

I can see approval being needed for the same reason as point one in this section, but I don't understand why it's not merely a formality or first-come, first-serve thing.

(They have a reputation for consistently denying requests because they don't want to set a precedent that might allow for more people to take off consecutive days.)

Moral dilemma:
- Be honest start to finish and possibly lose two days' worth of pay.
- Lie to their power-tripping faces (arguably a little harder to do now that I've let the proverbial cat out of the bag with my nosy questions).

Reasons why such policies are detrimental:
- Having to jump this many hoops and being regularly denied unless it's sudden and dire circumstances is sort of demoralizing.
- You're essentially training your people to lie to your face.

Internal ranting: We work in a school! We're supposed to be training a generation of upstanding citizens, and you've gone and made simple taking time off (which we have available to us) a moral question with a very tempting *lie-to-me* answer.

- From a certain point of view, you just stuck a price tag on integrity. That is many shades of uncool.

- (This, my non-teaching friends, is one of the reasons teachers feel mis-trusted.)

Philosophical cathartic musings:
- Taking the moral high ground has always been harder and pricier than compromising.
- I still have the option to appeal to the superintendent's good will.
- Being an adult sometimes comes with unfun choices. I'm still going, so if that's the price, that's the price.

Takeaways:
- Honesty's the best policy, but sometimes, it's also expensive and aggravating.
- This is a small example of how schools often function very differently than any other workplace.

Chapter 20:
Episode 80 – General Opinion: Covering Classes During Your Prep Period

Introduction:

Dear Reader,

It's not always the best policy to air the dirty laundry in public.

I also try to stay away from topics that are completely teaching-centric because I want the project as a whole to appeal to more than just teachers.

Let's talk about class coverages.

Other professions, like emergency workers, retail workers, restaurant workers, and surgeons have a plan in place for covering shifts if somebody calls out.

Most of the time, it's a whole shift, not just an hour, and the person stepping in would get paid accordingly.

The way the issue is handled in schools is unique and not entirely acceptable in some cases.

~Ann

The situation:
When a teacher calls out sick or takes a personal day at the last moment, sometimes the school calls in a substitute teacher.

However, there is often a shortage of substitute teachers for a variety of reasons.

When a substitute teacher cannot be found, schools don't usually have the luxury of closing a class for the day. (If a class is small enough—like 1-2 kids—they might be sent to the library for a period to have a study hall of sorts, but that's rare.)

That's where class coverages kick in.

Somebody—usually an overworked, underpaid, saint of a secretary—organizes the schedules and works out the puzzle of who has off on the right periods to be able to cover the class.

Pay for class coverages varies widely:
I haunted a few social media threads to get a feel for the situation. My ten-minute sleuthing exercise revealed the following tidbits:
- Some places in North Carolina, Kentucky, and Texas do not pay people for extra coverages. Teachers just take turns doing it.

Side note:
- Kentucky does not have a union, just an education association. The person who reported that also says they haven't had a decent raise in 10 years, but I don't know what they count as decent.
- California pays $75 per hour.
- These were some other hourly/class period wages I saw: $50, $12, $16, $37, $54, and $33.

- One person said the current rate was $15, but that is set to change over to $45 next year because the union negotiated it that way.
- I get $39 per hour.
- Many people said it's just expected of you.

The problem:
Let's review those numbers. $0 to $75. On the high end, that's a pretty reasonable deal that's tempting enough to get volunteers.

My school calls on volunteers, too. You have to indicate a willingness to do coverages.

Still, there are days when that extra prep period would be nice.

What does the teacher covering a class do?
Usually, it's just crowd control. Teachers are encouraged to leave lesson plans for the students, but if it's a true emergency, there may not even be that.

If the teacher is in the same content area, they might do some extra help with students or walk them through the review problems left by the regular teacher.

I usually get a lot of grading, reading, or phone game time logged when I'm covering a class.

The duties mostly involve taking attendance and giving students permission to use the restroom one at a time.

Options for handling being asked to do a class coverage:
- Just say no. It's easy advice to give, but this gets tricky if you are untenured.
- Reluctantly accept scenario 1 (external guilt trip): People are often guilt-tripped into accepting it. Essentially, the

administrator will scold the teacher for not being a *team player* if they turn down a coverage.

Side note: I kind of loath that term. Nothing good ever comes of it. If applied one way, it comes off as condescending. If applied a different way, it's generally euphemistic scolding.

- Reluctantly accept scenario 2 (internal guilt trip): Most reluctant souls, suck it up and do it anyway. They accept it as just another aspect of the job, as lesson planning is part of the job.
- Joyfully accept: Those of us who get paid decently might cringe a little at the lost mostly-me time (or the chance to eat), but we're mostly glad for the paycheck boost.

Side note 2: Please check your contracts. Some contracts prevent people from refusing coverages.

Friendly reminder: One person pointed out, that it stinks, but try not to complain to the secretary who is arranging the coverages. It's not his/her fault. That is a good point.

Points to consider (things that can make it worse):

- People take off regularly because districts don't always pay for unused Paid Time Off.
- There are also caps on what can be paid, so if they have 100 days saved up, people try very hard to use them.
- Some people are just slackers.

Short story aside: Once upon a time, there was a teacher who was late to school almost every day and another teacher had to cover for her. The covering teacher complained and the next year, the slacker had a prep period first, so if she was late, that's all she missed. The End.

The class coverage issue generates:

- Added stress
- Hard feelings

Possible solutions:

- Hire more substitute teachers – This may require paying them more.
- Pay teachers fairly for class coverage – Get rid of this unpaid, team player garbage. Money doesn't solve all problems, but it does sometimes put a bandage on added stress.

Note: A fair wage will differ district to district. I can't give one blanket number because not all numbers will line up with what's normal in that state. We can discuss teacher salaries in a future chapter.

Some general guidelines for what would constitute fair. If an entry-level job for unskilled labor would pay more, it's probably not fair. The $12 rate sounds like it was fair in 1956, and that's the last time someone bothered revisiting the number.

On the other hand, $75 per hour sounds nice, but I have no idea what district that's from. That could be hazard pay.

Takeaways:

- Classes need to be covered. Nobody disputes that point.
- It can be stressful to pull a class coverage.
- Getting paid to do a class coverage makes the inconvenience worth it to some people.
- Some people do not get much of a choice about doing a class coverage. That sounds wrong, but districts can get away with it if there is no union. (I am not the biggest union fan, but they do occasionally get some things right.)

Chapter 21:
Episode 81 – General Opinion (PSA): Advice for Students Part 1 – Avoid Pointless Comparisons

Introduction:

Dear Reader,

As we approach the end of the year, patience runs thin, and self-control wanes. It's time for some Public Service Announcements. The things discussed here apply all year round, but it's especially good to remember them in the final few weeks of the year.

Although I'll list as many as pop to mind, I probably don't have the space to elaborate on every single one of them.

Even if you are not personally a student, do your best to convey the message to those in your sphere, be they your children, your students, or your peers.

This is essentially *how to get your way without coming across as a self-righteous twit.*

~Ann

An important distinction:
Teachers are not bosses, but they fulfill a role of authority.

School is the perfect place for forming work habits and learning how to handle people.

I am not saying be manipulative, but there are certainly ways of handling yourself that will increase the likelihood of garnering favor with whoever is above you in the organizational caste system.

Back to the basics:
People—American's especially—cringe at the thought that not everything is equal.

Equal opportunity has never meant equal period, nor will it ever. People are different. Usually, that's a good thing.

There will always be some sort of system with leaders and followers by nature or by design.

For traditional schools to function, there needs to be rules, expectations, and people in charge of seeing that things get done.

Quick reminders:
- Teachers aren't the bad guys.
- Teachers bear the responsibility for learning. Often, arbitrary and random measuring tools (state tests) are used to gauge success. Officially, teachers answer to the administration, the district, and the state. Unofficially, they also work very hard to meet student and parent expectations.
- Authority and responsibility are inextricably linked.
- Teachers—typically—aren't glory hounds. There's a sense of triumph when something clicks with a student or a

lesson goes well. If the teacher's telling you something like put your phone away, it's generally not just to torture you.

Avoid comparisons of teachers, classes, or situations:

- Sample 1: Ms. X does this in her class. Why can't we do this?
- Sample 2: Mr. Y is a better teacher because he goes slower than you do.
- Sample 3: My English teacher lets us ...

My response:
Everyone is unique. It's unreasonable to expect teachers to handle situations in the same way.

One of my colleagues runs review sessions for the final starting about a month ahead of the end of the year. That's excellent. When we taught the same level, we would take turns doing the review sessions.

I chose not to do them this year. The key difference is that my colleague teaches honors classes. I do not have that level this year. Extra help is always available to my students in the middle of the week or any day before school. The influx of extra help seekers hits any test day, but that's it.

If my students truly cared to review, they would seek me out. They are more than welcome to do so, but I'm not going to plan something extra for them to blow it off or come once.

That's the difference between honors and general ed students.

Reality:

Every class is unique. There always a distinct mixture of students, teacher(s), and circumstances (time of day, number of students, type of students, etc.).

- Some classes have a co-teacher. Others do not.

- Some classes have the maximum number of students, and some have only a handful of students.
- Some classes are held in the morning. Others are held in the afternoon.
- Some schools have schedules where classes meet at the same time every day and others rotate some way.

The point is that every unique blend lends itself differently to things like how quickly material is covered, how well it gets covered, and even what sorts of privileges are extended to the students.

Things that work well in one kind of class do not work well in others. For example, the photography kids often spend whole class periods wandering the hallways. It's presumably in search of the perfect shot for a project. That kind of freedom is not great for most other classes.

Other observations:
- On the whole, small classes move through material faster.
- Behavior and how loud or quiet a class is also ties to how quickly the lessons get covered.
- It's harder to give one-to-one attention to every student if there are over twenty students in the class.

Teacher personalities differ:
- Some people are laid back. Kids can joke freely and address the teacher casually.
- Some prefer a relaxed atmosphere filled with color, light, and unicorn stickers everywhere.
- Other teachers like to run a tight ship.
- Some will let the class know clearly what sports teams they root for, what movies they watch, and what they intend to do on the weekend.
- Others prefer to stay a mystery.

- Some teachers love technology and will use every flashy new thing they can get their hands on.
- Others prefer to stick with older methods of doing things.

Some classes require a different touch:

My class rules are decidedly relaxed in the period where my students get their work done without arguing. They can listen to music more or play on their phones.

They get a lot more freedom because they've already seen to their work obligations for the course.

Additional point:

While this is mostly about comparing teachers and classes, I should add that students should not compare themselves to other students.

Everybody's life situation is unique.

Former Immigrant Student from Chapter 65 couldn't turn to her parents for help with school work. I had the luxury of asking my dad for help with chemistry and math.

- Some families can afford to pay for a tutor.
- Some families struggle to find their next meal.

Side note: Privilege is not a bad word. Acting entitled is a different matter, but privilege is merely an advantage one has. That's not inherently a bad thing. It's a part of life. There will always be people ahead of you in line and behind you. Use your skills to work your way forward as best you can.

The point is do the best you can with what you're given.
Being smart is only a very small piece of the equation that boils down to student success. Attitude also matters a lot, but I'll elaborate on that in the next chapter.

Takeaways:
- Don't compare teachers
- Don't compare classes
- Don't compare yourself to another student's situation

Chapter 22:
Episode 82 – General Opinion (PSA): Advice for Students Part 2 – Attitudes, Actions, and Things Not to Say

Introduction:

Dear Reader,

Last chapter focused more on the errant comparisons students make concerning teachers, classes, and each other.

This time, I'd like to concentrate on specific things students say, do, or take a hostile attitude about.

~Ann

Recap of privileges: (Ann plays Captain Obvious)

The smoother a class runs, the more privileges students get.

I can only speak for me, but here's how I work: I create lesson plans with a set amount of material to cover. Once the material is covered, students are free to play on their phones.

If getting the class settled is an epic battle, there's less time for the lesson itself. It therefore takes longer, leaves me with less patience, and students are less likely to receive privileges like handing their quizzes in once they finish.

Side note: You might not want to shout, "I'll just send you a picture of it." The it being your lab write up. I just laughed, but there's a good chance that statement goes poorly for you with another teacher.

Avoid pointless blanket statements:
- We're all going to fail the final.

My response: With that crappy attitude, it's likely. Maybe change your attitude.

(They're not all going to fail the final unless they spend the entirety of their prep time on their phones and complaining to each other that they know nothing. Then, it's possible, but even then, *they* are not the whole class.)

Avoid demands, declarations, and informing:
- I'm getting a drink.
- I'm going to the restroom.

My response: Both are quite reasonable requests to make, though do try to avoid making them every day then staying out for ten minutes at a time.

Side note: I have heard of teachers refusing to let kids use the restroom. I don't bother, but I do see their point. Some kids go for 10-13 minute "restroom" breaks that really involve a brief stop in the restroom, a leisurely stroll to the water fountain, and a walk around every hallway in the school on the way back. That's excessive and unnecessary for 99.99% of the kids.

(There's always a rare kid with an actual medical condition that requires frequent bathroom visits. That is not what we're discussing here.)

- I'm texting my dad because my Great Aunt died.

My response: I'm sorry to hear that but informing me of that isn't the best move. Asking for permission to text about a family matter is a much better way to handle it.

PSA for parents: A loss in the family is tragic. Texting students in class is disruptive, regardless of the reason.

I'm not saying there is never a reason to text your child. I am asking you to consider what messages you are sending them both literally and by example.

Kids often say, "I'm texting my mom" like it's a valid excuse. It is usually not.

There was a time before every kid had a cellphone permanently superglued to their hand, and people still stayed in touch as needed. Family is important, but there is a time for everything. Despite what students think, they do have down time in between classes. A 20-minute delay in a text is not going to make or break the majority of situations being texted about.

(The kid didn't seem that broken up over the loss. That too could make a difference. If someone was truly distraught over a loss, they should go to guidance to get the help they need.)

And some of the times students claim to be texting their mom they're also playing a video game. I wasn't born yesterday. I know they lie to my face instinctively.

- I need to call my mom. It's an emergency.

My response: (I actually had this conversation with a student today.) When pressed about the emergency, it turned out he needed his mom to bring him his lunch and some cream for a leg injury.

While those might be important things, they do not qualify as an emergency. (For the record, an emergency is something we're ready to call 911 for.) If this kid doesn't learn that distinction, he'll risk becoming the boy who cried wolf.

- I need to text my mom to arrange for a ride after school.

My response: Also had this conversation today. (Was an interesting day for conversations.) This student is constantly on her phone. She asked for permission to text her mom for a ride. Twenty minutes later, she was on her phone again. I asked her to put it down for about the 50th time that class period. She responded (with a poor attitude) that she was getting a reply from her mom about the ride.

The messages don't go away. It'll still be there after the ten minutes I want to spend on a lesson.

Captain Obvious Strikes Again:
Attitude is almost everything.

Asking goes a long way, but even getting permission to send one text isn't a pass for the entire period.

Responding like a brat is not going to get you any points in the goodwill category.

Things you need goodwill for:
- Permission to text your mom about your lunch or a ride or leg cream.
- Permission to get a drink (and take a walk).
- Permission to use the restroom instantly every single time you ask no matter how many times you ask in a class period.
- Permission to step out and finish eating breakfast.
- Permission to hand in homework a few hours late or the next day for whatever reason.

That adage about gathering more flies with honey holds true.

Attitude is going to be a very large factor in how somebody is going to want to respond to you.

Most requests are easily granted. I trust (most) of my students aren't on a mission to waste their time and mine.

The most common reason for asking someone to wait is that there are too many people out of the room. A close second is that I'm about to give some important instructions.

Takeaways:

- Use your time wisely.
- Asking usually makes people want to grant your request.
- Avoid pointless blanket statements like *we're all going to fail*.
- Take your attitude issues outside the school. Nobody deserves to be sniped at. Your family might tolerate it, but a teacher should not have to deal with that. It does not win you any goodwill.

Chapter 23:
Episode 83 – General Opinion: Senseless and Sensationalism – Thoughts on School Shootings

Introduction:

Dear Reader,

Columbine, Colorado. Newtown, Connecticut. Parkland, Florida. Santa Fe, Texas. These are four of a frighteningly long list of school shooting incidents since 1999.

They're most notable because they're some of the deadliest.

Truthfully, not all of the incidents even make national news. Most just disappear after a few hours on a local news site because not enough people died to make it memorable.

As of Tuesday, May 24, 2022, there's a new town name to add to the list: Uvalde, Texas. The numbers are still fluctuating, but well over a dozen students and at least one teacher died.

The articles I read indicated that today was the second to last day of school for the year. Somehow, that tidbit adds another emotional smack to the mix.

This is not a type of fame any town wants.

It's a touchy, emotion-filled topic. I'm going to continue with it, but if it's just upsetting you, maybe don't read this one.

~Ann

What happened (the super short version based on the articles):
A young man barged into an elementary school and went classroom to classroom unleashing pain, panic, and death with a gun.

(What type of gun, how many he had, the exact path he took through the school and so forth will be established over the next few days and weeks as the police and FBI investigate.)

The articles focused mainly on the loss of young lives. The adults are mentioned almost as an afterthought.

What happens now?
- The authorities in Uvalde will be very, very busy.
- As will the funeral homes.
- Flower sales will shoot up (balloons, cards, catering, etc.).
- The wounded will recover in hospitals and at home. They may have emotional fallout for a while or forever. (survivor's guilt, nightmares, other trauma)
- People will argue.
- Gun sales will skyrocket.
- Interest in school shootings will spike. Google searches on the topic will increase. Books on the topic both fiction and nonfiction may also see a bump.
- Prayers and tears will flow.
- Pastors will work it into their sermons.

- Counselors are going to be busy.
- Kids and teachers will mourn the loss of life and innocence and the illusion of peace.
- The nation will gawk at the articles written about it. Some will mourn. Some will shake their heads. Some will just shrug and move on with their lives.

General note: Of the things listed, there's no right or wrong way to react. There's always the hope that we can salvage something good from this.

I just witnessed one of the typical discussions that unfolded on social media. I'll recount it to the best of my abilities.

Explanation: I am only going to pull sentiments, not direct quotes. I am quite certain if I looked at a few dozen other posts, they would say much the same thing.

Grab a drink and sit down. It's going to be a familiar conversational ride.

The comments are going to be in a random order, though I tried to group by opposites.

Side note: This came from a group of educators.

Summary of the social media posts about the Uvalde school shooting:
- Many people: I am confused and sad and disheartened.
- We should pray for them.
- Prayers don't work, change the laws!
- We should do something!
- What exactly would you like done?
- Guns don't kill people; people kill people. (But guns make it easier for people to kill people.)

- Cars kill more people than guns, are you saying we get rid of cars?
- Call your senators. Make them do something.
- It's the Republicans fault.
- It's the Democrats fault.
- Why does it always turn political?
- It's nobody's fault except the killer.
- It's those gun lovers.
- It's those mentally ill psychos.
- Where'd this eighteen-year-old get the guns he used to murder a dozen plus people?
- Say the killer's name, remember him as a bad, bad man.
- Don't give the perpetrator the five seconds of fame.
- Give teachers guns!
- More guns are not the answer!
- Guns are part of the problem.
- Guns are NOT the problem.
- Mental health is the issue.
- Stop blaming mental health!
- Hey, technology is a factor too. And parenting. Crappy parenting is a problem too.
- You're stupid.
- No, you're stupid.
- Can't we all just get along?
- Stricter gun laws. That's the answer!
- Do your dang research, the criminals don't pay any attention to gun laws.
- Mental illness is the ultimate culprit
- I don't think he was mentally ill. I think he just snapped.
- Medications come with side effects that include hallucinations.
- There will be an uptick in homeschooling.

- We need to teach more conflict resolution and empathy.
- Teaching empathy is a parenting thing. Don't you dare add one more thing to my plate.

What will likely happen now:

By the time this publishes on June 2, 2022, the story will be on its way out of the headlines. There will likely be a surge because that's within the window of time for funerals to be happening.

The town's earned its black mark of infamy. It will be emotionally reeling for a while.

The rest of the nation will move on, eventually letting it fade behind a new tragic headline.

There probably will be some laws changed. It may be sweeping, but it's more likely that it'll change one small thing and make things inconvenient while still managing to do zero real good. Maybe that's the cynic in me coming out.

General reflections:

There's no single right reaction to have. So, if you're feeling stuff, let the emotions happen. Bottling them will make matters worse. Everybody blaming something is likely falling into a blind-men-describe-an-elephant situation. (The moral of that story is that people describe only the small portion they're experiencing.)

Guns, meds, depression, mental illness, failure of parents, failure of society, obsession with technology, sin and depravity of mankind in general, and much more bear some of the blame.

Asking *how much blame each should bear* is a pointless exercise. The facts remain that a young man with access to weapons made a choice that drastically changed a few hundred lives, a small town is cast into the limelight in the worst way possible, some people will profit from the tragedy, and healing will happen in time.

What should you do? (Possible takeaways):
Your personal response should be what you feel moved to do.

- Additional prayers are never wasted.
- I'm sure there will be gofundme and other charity things cropping up if you feel you should help financially.
- If all you get out of this is the notion to cherish your loved ones more, that's fine.
- If you're galvanized to change a law you think is failing your town or country, go for it.

Chapter 24:
Episode 84 – Special Guest: Conflicted Academic Reacts to School Shootings

Introduction:
Dear Reader,

School shootings are some of the most heartbreaking, morbidly fascinating phenomenon of the whole educational soup.

The previous discussion went deeper into general thoughts and reactions.

This time, we'll (the royal we) be speaking with one brave soul conflicted about the common reactions (blaming guns, mental health, etc.).

~Ann

What would you like to be called?
Let's go with Conflicted Academic. I feel like I'm seeing many different sides to the subject, and they don't always mesh nicely together.

Can you tell me a bit about your background?
Conflicted Academic: I work at a large university library in the archives.

I've always been big in history and the context of things, which has made it so that I see things as varying shades of gray. Stuff isn't black and white, and it never has been.

Is there a difference between summer and normal academic school year work?
Conflicted Academic: Summer has less traffic is all.

A lot of the people on campus who don't directly work with students use the summer to catch up on various projects that aren't 100% student related, such as fundraising.

We technically have classes during the summer, but there are a lot less students.

You mentioned there are multiple sides to you and things don't always mesh well. Can you please elaborate on that?
Conflicted Academic: One part of me is the parent who would do anything to protect my kids.

I've experienced being the victim in school violence (severe bullying), and I don't ever want my kids (or any kids) to experience that feeling of helplessness.

Feel free to elaborate on the bullying part if you like. I am here to listen, learn, and share, but no pressure either way. You do what's comfortable for you.
Conflicted Academic: I appreciate that. The other part is the side of me that grew up around guns and **safe** gun culture.

While my parents didn't have guns in the house growing up, I had extended family and friends whose family that did, and so, I learned about how to treat guns with respect and not use them to hurt others. They should only be used in self-defense.

What are your thoughts on violence in schools?

Conflicted Academic: As for school violence growing up, I was actually pulled from my elementary school in first grade because there were kids who were threatening to hurt me because they were angry with the world, and I was the easiest target.

Me: Well, that's scary.

Conflicted Academic: I was homeschooled until high school, and even then, there was bullying, but I could usually escape it by hanging out with my teachers or staying in the school library.

My mother said she was afraid every day that she'd get a call from the school telling her that something had happened to me. (Not that life at home with her was much better, but that's a different story.) Obviously, as a six-year-old, I didn't understand the gravity of the situation, only that most of the kids didn't like me.

Most kids who bully others pick on something inane that's different. Can you pinpoint the thing that was different that they targeted you for?

Conflicted Academic: There are a few things that could possibly be the reason.

My home life was not loving. My mother is a narcissist, so I grew up seeking love and a place to fit in.

I didn't always push back when kids would bully me, because my mother had ingrained in me that I was the 'bad kid' so if I did push back, I was afraid I'd get in trouble. Both with other kids and adults.

My dad worked and traveled a lot during this time, so he was usually away on business trips and what not.

Another reason is that I was always the *weird kid*. I'm 99.9% sure I'm neurodivergent and that's never a good thing in school with other kids.

Me: *heads to Google to figure out what the heck neurodivergent is.* Oh, I've heard the term before. It basically means what it says in the word. A person's brain works differently than what is usually accepted as normal.

On Tuesday, May 24, 2022 there was yet another school shooting. You indicated that the event kind of threw you for a loop. Can you explain the mixed emotions it stirred?

Conflicted Academic: When I first heard the news, I got sick to my stomach.

My oldest is in kindergarten and it would destroy me if I found out something like this had happened to her (or any of my other kids when they are school aged).

So immediately my heart went out to the parents who are now grieving their children and planning funerals instead of summer fun with those kids.

People are quick to place blame for school violence on guns. What are your thoughts on that?

Conflicted Academic: I knew that people would start yelling about banning guns and how *mass killings* aren't an issue in other countries.

And growing up with people who used guns properly (i.e., not to murder others), I knew this would anger me as well. In my mind, guns aren't the problem.

Culture and mediocre mental health services are the problem, in my opinion.

Guns are a tool. Just like fertilizer (can be used to make bombs). Just like cars. Just like planes. Just like kitchen knives and the chemicals used to make stuff like ricin.

Random side note: I am a writer. I was using a giant, very sharp knife on a tomato today, and I was like: *oooohhhh, this is a really nice knife; it would make a great murder weapon.*

Conflicted Academic: I've had that same experience. I fenced in high school and briefly in college and had a very interesting experience with a friend about my fencing sword.

Me: Yay. I'm not the only one. (I've told exactly two people that—both writers—who admitted to similar lines of thoughts.)

Is there an answer for this kind of problem (shooting violence in schools)?
Conflicted Academic: Yes and no.

Is there an easy answer to shooting violence in schools or in general, no. There isn't a simple or easy one. As much as I'd love one.

So, what do you think are tough answers that may be achievable eventually?
Conflicted Academic: Mental health is a BIG thing to me.

We need more training, research, and acceptance of people seeking out mental health services at all ages.

I'd even say having more & BETTER in-patient institutions.

Do you have any other closing thoughts for this section?
Conflicted Academic: Merely that shooting violence isn't something that has a simple answer. And I don't think I have the perfect solution or solutions. Far from it. I just know that (from

studying history) it's going to take a lot of small, local solutions to change things. And they may not change that much during our lifetimes, unfortunately.

Takeaways:

- There is no one fix-all solution to the problem of public shootings and school shootings.
- Each town and city will have to improve things as a whole, including services for those struggling with mental health issues. (That is NOT saying that mental health is the only factor contributing to school shootings.)

Chapter 25:
Episode 85 – Special Guest:
Alternative Schooling Advocate

Introduction:

Dear Reader,

Education encompasses many things, but typically, when people talk about the education system, they're referring to the public school system.

While individual triumphs certainly happen, the American public school system struggles in several key ways.

This chapter won't deep-dive into let's count the many ways the public school system is failing its mandate to teach the next generation, but it will touch upon some of the issues.

Our next guest is also the previous guest (Conflicted Academic). This time, she's speaking to us as an Alternative Schooling Advocate and offering more glimpses into her schooling experiences.

I think I've mentioned how unexpectedly difficult it is to get people to talk about their personal school experiences. My guess is that this stems from those who liked school feeling they have nothing to add and those who disliked school not wanting to talk about it for a variety of reasons.

~Ann

What do you mean by alternative schooling?
Alternative Schooling Advocate: Anything that isn't going to a public school. This covers private school, boarding school, homeschool, virtual or online school, night school, and so forth.

Disclaimer: I am aware that public school systems vary very widely based on the socioeconomic status of the district.

What are your issues with the public school system?
Alternative Schooling Advocate:
The main problems I see:
- Bureaucracy
- Lack of funding for pretty much anything beyond the bare minimum
- Testing! I had SOLs (standards of learning) and those were soul-sucking for students and teachers alike.

Me: Those slippery suckers change their name every few years and vary by state, but yeah, agreed, completely soul draining.

Alternative Schooling Advocate: One of the benefits of being outside of public school is that my love of learning last longer than my sisters who were in public school for all of their K-12 education.

I got to explore the subjects I loved with more depth, whereas they were burnt out by anything school related by graduation.

You told us a little about your early schooling experiences—the ones that prompted homeschooling for a while—is there anything you'd like to add to

that?

Alternative Schooling Advocate: Not too much. I craved my teachers' approval when I was younger, but due to the previously mentioned neurodivergent issues and problems at home, I struggled socially with my peers.

It was easier to talk to adults than kids.

Me: Kids can be difficult to talk to. They're learning how to interact with each other, and some of them do not master the how-to-function-in-public-without-being-a-jerk lesson until much later in life. (If society can be judged, sadly, some never master that lesson, but perhaps that's overly cynical.)

You mentioned quite a few alternative schooling options. Among those, do you have a preference?
Alternative Schooling Advocate: My experience was mainly with homeschooling or public schooling, but I had friends who did a hybrid of both and sometimes I wish I had done that.

Some of my friends did private school, and I taught at a boarding school in China for a semester. Some kids thrived in those situations, while others did not.

Me: That statement is going to prompt more nosy questions. Prepare yourself. I'll come back to them.

What kind of student were you? (Describe yourself as a student in elementary, middle, and high school. I'm interested in your metamorphosis.)
Alternative Schooling Advocate: I wanted to learn and grow as much as possible. The library and classrooms were my safe places from the world. So, I wanted to learn and please my teachers as much as possible.

Me: Guess it's not surprising that you ended up working in a library.

Do you feel your high school prepared you for the real world?
Alternative Schooling Advocate: Not really.
Me: No hesitation whatsoever. Guess that's clear enough.

What lessons would you have liked to learn?
Alternative Schooling Advocate:
- I really wish they'd made a financial literacy program mandatory.
- My school had a culinary arts program, but that was an elective. Having at least one mandatory class on the basics of cooking would have helped a lot of my classmates.
- Internet and information literacy.

Personal reflection: I think we had home economics class but that mostly boiled down to basic sewing. Guess this is why I can sew a mean button on and mostly eat spaghetti when left to my own devices.

If you were given complete control, a very large budget, and a year to change the public school system for the better, what changes would you implement?
Alternative Schooling Advocate:
- Improve the pay and benefits of teachers and ensure that the increase is a permanent line increase.
- Low pay and minimal benefits doesn't do anything for teachers.

Me: You might be my new best friend.
- More support and supplies inside and outside the school as well.

Me: Pencils. So. Many. Pencils.

- Ensure food security for students without cost. A lot of students in my area rely on school for daily meals.

Me: That's sad. I know there are ways the schools can continue to provide meals over breaks, but I wonder if everybody who qualifies takes advantage of the program.

Takeaways: Do you have any advice for students?
Alternative Schooling Advocate:
- Learning isn't just in the classroom. Learning happens everywhere.
- Just because mainstream education styles don't work for you doesn't mean you are dumb.
- You just need to find how you learn best.
- Also, it's never too late to learn something new.

Chapter 26:
Episode 86 – Special Guest: Semester Abroad English Teacher

Introduction:
Dear Reader,

In recent weeks, I've become more appreciative of how broad the topic of education can truly be.

The last guest mentioned that she taught at a boarding school in China for a semester while in college.

Of course, that prompted me to pry.

~Ann

What made you decide to teach abroad? How did that even come about?
Semester Abroad English Teacher: I originally did it because I wanted to do Study Abroad, but that fell through, so I went to a meeting for an organization called ILP (International Language Programs).

(They had free pizza, and I was a poor college student.)

Me: Ah, the old pizza trap. I see.

Semester Abroad English Teacher: They had a program where you teach oral English overseas.

Initially their programs were in China and Russia, but now they are in a variety of countries, but not China or Russia due to geopolitical stuff.

Me: According to their website, the current countries are Lithuania, Mexico, Thailand, and Ukraine. (Might I suggest not going to Ukraine right now.)

What was the application process like?
Semester Abroad English Teacher: I filled out an application and told them what semester would work for me. Then I did a few training sessions with them, and they took care of everything else (i.e., visas).

Me: I looked them up. (Yes, it was Google because I'm lazy, and that's what my search engine defaulted to.) They tout their program as "including housing, food, roundtrip international airfare from the US and Canada, visa and culture experiences." (**https://blog.ilp.org-which-ilp-program-is-best-for-you**)

Their website emphasizes the fact that this is a service abroad, not study abroad, thing.

Did you pay for the experience?
Semester Abroad English Teacher: Yes, it was about $2500 for a semester, but that took care of airline tickets, transportation to and from the school and costs for visas.

I went a second time as a head teacher and my expenses were paid for by ILP, but that's because head teachers are in charge of 6-7 student teachers.

What was your first impression of the country?

Semester Abroad English Teacher: First Impression of China –
It's massive and simultaneously similar and very different than the
United States.

- Similar in that people are people. A lot of the people I met
  and knew in China had similar feelings, desires, and
  experiences to people I knew from home.
- Different in the things that they put emphasis on, history,
  culture of doing stuff for the group vs. individualism.

What was the most fun part about the experience?

Semester Abroad English Teacher: Exploring, meeting new
friends from all around China, and trying new things.

What was the most difficult part about the experience?

Semester Abroad English Teacher: Language and culture
differences, such as the mentality of not questioning work
exploitation. Having to work ten to twelve hours per day unpaid
when our contract was for two to three hours of teaching for five
days a week.

How did you prepare the lessons?

Semester Abroad English Teacher: ILP has their own
curriculum, so we'd create lesson plans for the week and have the
head teacher check them off, then we'd gather supplies for our
various projects.

What kind of projects?

Semester Abroad English Teacher: Arts & Crafts, theater,
music, physical education.

The curriculum was based around learning English through play
and practicing the language in real time.

Did you get close to any of the kids you taught?

Semester Abroad English Teacher: Yes and no. Most of the kids we taught were elementary school age (even preschool age), so we'd have students that we enjoyed having in our classes, but after we returned home, we didn't necessarily keep in touch.

That said, I have a picture of one of our students that I absolutely love, even fifteen years later.

Me: *sees picture. Kid kind of looks like he's giving you the bird.
Semester Abroad English Teacher: He's not actually flipping us off. He was trying to do a peace sign while wearing the teacher's watch and hat, both of which were waaaay too big for him.

Did you get set days off to explore?
Semester Abroad English Teacher: We did. I went in the Fall so we got a week at the beginning of October to travel as well as a three-day weekend each month.

Would you do it again if you had the chance?
Semester Abroad English Teacher: Absolutely. I highly recommend it to college-aged kids and friends all the time.

Do you think you learned anything through the experience?
Semester Abroad English Teacher:
- I learned that the vast majority of people are the same deep down even if we come from very different places.
- I related more to some of my Chinese co-teachers than some of my American co-teachers.
- I also learned that sometimes the *bad kid* isn't bad, so much as their skills haven't been found yet.
- We had one student who was very disruptive until he became the teacher's helper. Then he was respectful and a quick learner, and a general joy in class.
- Actually, we had a few kids like that. They were labeled as troublesome, but once we figured how to connect with them, they were great students.

What's your pitch for college kids who might be on the fence about trying something like this?

Semester Abroad English Teacher: This experience is something you'll always remember and it's something that you'll get as much out of as you put in.

I've had a lot of amazing experiences teaching, both inside and outside the classroom.

That said, it's definitely not for the faint of heart.

Me: I demand—I mean I feel like that point needs some elaboration.

What makes you say that?

Semester Abroad English Teacher: As a teacher, you're dealing with kids coming from every type of background, even in private schools or other school situations.

And sometimes being a teacher means more than making sure your kids know their subjects.

Sometimes it means advocating for them, mentoring them, or just being a positive influence, even if they don't initially know that they need or want those things. So, it can be an emotionally grueling job.

Me: Yes, that is a lesson one learns while teaching. I got so wrapped up in the experience part and forgot that it was a first-year teaching job too.

Takeaways:
- Teaching abroad can be tough.
- Teaching abroad is an excellent experience.
- Teaching abroad lets college students learn about a different culture.

Chapter 27:
Episode 87: Special Guest: Hard-Working History Teacher Part 1

Introduction:

Dear Reader,

I think this might be the first history teacher I tracked down. (It's not for lack of trying. I do the equivalent of shout on social media street corners.)

The humanities are a different world than the one I'm used to dealing with, but it's no surprise that the issues facing teachers are applicable across subjects.

Before we dive into issues and advice, let's get to know this guest.

~Ann

Welcome. What would you like me to call you?

Hard-Working History Teacher.

Me: That works for me. Awesome. Let's get started.

How many years did you teach?

Hard-Working History Teacher: I just finished year sixteen. Year seventeen starts in August.

Side note: Many schools start in August and end in May. The other half start September and end in June. (I'm in the half going to June.)

Did you have a different career?

Hard-Working History Teacher: I thought I might want to go to law school after college, so I worked as a project assistant at a law firm dealing with discovery tort.

I didn't find it appealing after a few months, so I decided to go back and get a Masters in Education while working this job.

I worked in the legal field for 2.5 years. I hated the work I had to do and be around, but it definitely pointed me to the right direction. **Me:** Ah, another late-blooming teacher. I didn't embark upon the path until the end of college. It's always fascinating to see the many paths that lead into and out of teaching as a career.

Did you have friends in high school?

Hard-Working History Teacher: I did. I was in the nerdy/academic crowd, but I had a couple good friends that were older than me.

We'd always play basketball growing up because I was a sports fanatic.

Me: School is a great place to locate people with similar interests. I believe another guest mentioned something about similar interests (Chapter 56).

Did you get close to any teachers when you were a student?

Hard-Working History Teacher: My biology teacher and my Algebra II teacher were my favorites as a student.

The biology teacher was my Quiz Bowl coach and sort of a confidante on things going on in life. She was just an amazing person.

The Algebra II teacher was the head basketball coach and a good math teacher. He made school fun and was probably the goofiest teacher I had in high school.

I appreciated the fact that it wasn't always business in the classroom.

A few teachers always stayed with me.

I went to the high school I taught at for the first fourteen years of my teaching career.

Interesting. What was that like? Did you teach with people you knew as a student?

Hard-Working History Teacher: During my first couple of years, some of my favorites were still there or hanging around.

My coach for Academic Decathlon was the physics teacher. (I never took physics in high school.) He was one of my mentors during my first year, then he left to become an assistant principal and then a principal.

My language arts teachers for my last three years of high school are still in communication with me. They were so good at making me a better writer that I just appreciated them so much.

I still get a Christmas/winter break card from one of them on her trips all over the world.

Me: That's great. Traveling is exhausting, but it can also be exciting.

And writing is indeed a wonderful gift. I don't think I could teach it, but I have gotten a lot of good things from the ability to write.

Guess that means I should go and thank my middle school English teacher.

Why did you choose teaching?
Hard-Working History Teacher: I was lost in college. I was pre-med then wanted to go to law school. I had no clue.

Two parts of my life really helped me to solidify that I wanted to be a teacher.

First, I worked at a kids' camp in Massachusetts for two summers. That was the best non-career type job I ever had. I liked working with kids and teaching them about life, being almost a parental figure since we were with them for 7-8 weeks straight.

That started to get the wheels turning.

Second, I was a Sunday School youth group teacher for two years. That was fun getting to know older kids (eighth and ninth grade) and guiding them through life as well.

I learned about having a lesson ready every week on top of my job. Many of those kids I still keep in touch with. Those two times plus my love of history catapulted me into choosing a Masters program in social studies right by my workplace, and I never turned back.

How long does it take you to prepare for a class?
Hard-Working History Teacher: Now, it takes a little bit of time to prep for lessons because I've figured out that coming up with my own plan that might not be as good as someone else's is most likely a waste of time.

I feel like I know the material very well.

Back when I started, it took me three to four hours a day. I had to go over the material then come up with notes and an activity.

I'd wake up early in the morning (like 4:30-5:00 a.m.) because class began at 7:20 a.m. when I first started. I would make copies for my kids for the notes and activity then have class then rinse and repeat.

On top of all that, I was the cross-country coach and had to prep for that since I would have practice right after school.

After practice when the kids went home, I would start planning again (at 4:30). Some days, I wouldn't be done planning until 10:00 p.m.

One day during my first year, I stayed in my classroom trailer so late, the local police knocked on my trailer to see who was in there. It was almost midnight and very embarrassing.

Me: That must have been kind of startling and scary. (I do not miss first-year of teaching.)

Takeaways:
- There is no one right way to end up in the teaching profession.
- Preparing for class can take many hours, but it does get easier over time.

Chapter 28:
Episode 88 – Special Guest: Hard-Working History Teacher Part 2 – Preps

Introduction:
Dear Reader,

We'd just started chatting about preps when the last chapter ended. We're going to pick right up there, so I'll turn it back over to our guest.

~Ann

Side note clarification for non-teachers that's probably really late:
Prep can have two meanings.

- It can mean a course the teacher would have to prepare lesson plans for.
- It can also mean the act of preparing lessons for a class, depending on context.

How do you approach prep?

Hard-Working History Teacher: Prep is important, but you can prep all you want and if the kids aren't getting it or need some remediation, then you have to be able to ad lib your plans.

I was not as malleable as a teacher until year ten or so.

Me: I think that—not being adaptable as a teacher—is fairly common, though I guess that depends on personality.

Hard-Working History Teacher: I was very anxiety driven, if plans did not go through like I wanted. Now, my colleague and I have a game plan for the whole year, but it's not too rigid and has space for change if needed for snow days, relearning, testing, etc. Nowadays, if I were to have to teach strictly from a topic given to me last second, I could put something together very quickly.

What kind of school did/do you work in?

Hard-Working History Teacher: For my first fourteen years, I taught at a Title I suburban school.

We had sports and clubs with mostly Hispanic and African American students. We had a sprinkling of Asian students and very few White students.

For the last two years, I have been at a STEM school. It is also Title I and suburban. There is no lottery to get in as students nearby and those with permissive transfers can get in pending administration approval.

We do not have sports, but they can play for their home school. We do have clubs.

We have mostly Hispanic students with some African American, Asian, and White students mixed in.

What classes did/do you teach?

Hard-Working History Teacher: When I first started, I taught

World History.

I have also taught American Government, Contemporary Issues, Geography, US History, Advanced Placement (AP) US History, and AP European History.

Currently, I teach US History and AP US History.

I enjoy these classes the most of any that I've ever taught.

What was the most preps you had in a year?
Hard-Working History Teacher: Three. I taught US History, AP US History, and AP European History in one year.

Usually, I have two. Only in my World History days did I ever have one prep.

Me: One prep is a beautiful thing, but it is very rare.

What was your favorite class to teach?
Hard-Working History Teacher: AP US History and AP European History because of the depth I get to go into these topics and the level of conversation I get to have with students. Plus, I love it when I hear students got college credit from my class.

(I do like my on-level students a ton as well. We also have great conversations.)

What was your favorite topic to teach?
Hard-Working History Teacher: I vacillate on this topic a lot. I think my favorite topic has to be any time we talk about change that happened in this country.

I like talking about how America goes through each phase from colonial times to new nation, Civil War to industrial power, lack of social reform from government to government help to the people, or isolationist to interventionist.

If I have to narrow it down to one topic, I like the Gilded Age because that's where America became such a power, but it hurt so many people at the same time.

The Gilded Age was pretty on the outside but ugly on the inside.
Me: That seems to be the way of most things. Pretty outside, ugly inside is a sobering thought.

What was your least favorite class to teach?
Hard-Working History Teacher: Geography. It wasn't the topic. I love geography. I disliked the fact that I got a brand-new class one month into the school year with freshmen from three different classes for a subject I had never taught.

I had never taught freshmen and probably will not teach them again if I can help it. That class was a mess.

Me: Props for those who teach freshman. I did that once upon a time. Yeah, I'd like to avoid that too.

What is the best, worst, and most fun part of teaching?
Hard-Working History Teacher:
- The best is when students improve in class and get excited about it or come back to you after they've been away for a year or longer and tell you what they've been up to or how you helped them out.
- The worst is dealing with classroom management issues or when you feel you don't have the support of your administration.

(Bonus worst)
- Another one that might be worse if when you have to deal with students who have issues beyond your control outside of school, and they have a hard time dealing with it in your class. (I.e., mental health issue, death in family, a friend died, a bad injury.)

- The most fun part is when students are enjoying your class and doing well. That is fun for me.

Are you involved in any extracurriculars as a teacher?

Hard-Working History Teacher: Yes.

- I have been a cross-country coach for five years.
- I coached Academic Decathlon for fourteen years
- I have helped out with Quiz Bowl for about four or five years.

What is the biggest downside of coaching or doing extracurriculars?

Hard-Working History Teacher: I enjoyed them, but athletic coaching is time-consuming. Also, if you have good teams in any type of competition, then it is horribly time-consuming.

When do you think the emphasis on grades kicks in?

Hard-Working History Teacher: I think it starts in middle school, but then, it really kicks in during their freshman year because they realize that they need to do well to go to this college. Grade Point Average (GPA) and class rankings also kick in.

They don't understand it until it's too late in high school. It's kind of a shame all the way around. A lot of times, I think it can be too much especially for students not trying to go to an elite school.

Takeaways:

- Extracurricular activities are awesome but time consuming.
- Seeing kids interested in your class is a wonderful feeling.
- Classroom management is one of the un-fun parts of teaching.
- The quality of administration can make or break teachers. (They need to feel supported.)

Chapter 29:
Episode 89 – Special Guest: Hard-Working History Teacher Part 3 – Advice and Reflections

Introduction:
Dear Reader,

We've covered the background and details for how Hard-Working History Teacher approaches his job.

Now, let's get to the advice and reflections portions of the interview.

~Ann

What do you think kids need to succeed at school?
Hard-Working History Teacher:
- Parental support
- Teacher support
- Just support in general

Me: Although I'm tempted to ask which of those you (and the readers) think is the most important, it's not really a fair question. All three are vitally important.

Can you elaborate on that? What kinds of things can teachers do to help students?
Hard-Working History Teacher:
- We as teachers can talk to our students and see how they are doing.
- They can tell if you care about them.
- The more you invest in them as people, then the more they will invest in your class.
- Students who know I care for them will run through a brick wall for me.

Do you have any concerns about education?
Hard-Working History Teacher: I think we need to make sure kids can read and write as they move up from elementary to high school.

Sometimes, students just move up grade levels, and as a high school teacher, I have a hard time understanding how that happens.

Do you have any advice for new teachers?
Hard-Working History Teacher:
- Get some great mentors and examples.
- Observe as many people as you can teach because there's no one way to be a good teacher.
- Don't try to wing it on your own.
- Take advice well and have a great team to work with.
- Being alone your first year is not fun.
- Make teacher friends and network as much as possible.
- Never ever burn any bridges because you never know when you might need a friend years down the road.

Me: We could spend the entire chapter just unpacking those points. All of that is excellent advice.

Taking advice with grace can be very difficult.

Teacher friends are the best because they know exactly what you're going through and have likely been there before.

How did the pandemic affect teaching?
Hard-Working History Teacher:
General points:
- Spring 2020 was the worst semester of teaching I have ever had.
- We weren't prepared.
- Going full digital that semester and having Zoom/Google Meets meetings was rough.
- Students did not learn.
- Only the determined (and those that had technology) wanted to do school, but it was understandably a rough time for many.
- The next year, I had concurrent learning where some were digital, and some were in-person.
- Luckily, I had just moved to a new school that knew how to use technology and digital resources, so I learned a ton from my new colleagues.

Me: The hybrid teaching year (half the kids virtual (digital) and half in-person) was a very strange time. I did enjoy some things about the schedule, but it was stressful to get an ever-changing schedule.

My school had given all students chromebooks the previous year, but dodgy internet connections were still an issue.

Points concerning students:
- Students who came in-person learned, but some seemed understandably distant.
- Some at home were comfortable with a digital platform

because we're a STEM school, yet others disappeared due to no home internet connection or other issues that were beyond our control.

Points concerning educators:

- I flipped some of my lessons for questions and answers, so they weren't just staring at me to say something.
- At my school, I feel many did their best. Teachers did their best to try and teach to a class or a computer screen, but it came to be too much for some.
- Because of these issues, I see that teachers got burnt out quickly as administrators or local school officials would say one protocol then change it to another.
- I have seen more teachers and people in education leave our profession in the last two years than I had seen in my fourteen years prior (or at least it seems like it).
- Many of them are young, vibrant professionals who want to do something else, and others are just tired and want nothing to do with what they see as a mess at their school.
- (Note: I have many teacher friends, so this is not a shot at my current school because I currently like it there).
- It bothers me to no end.

Me: I think a lot of teachers had to adjust somehow. We weren't allowed to do hands-on labs last year, so there was a lot more virtual labs and simulations and activities. They're okay, but the ability to touch stuff in a lab is one of the rites of passage the last batch of students missed out on for the year.

Do you have any closing thoughts about teaching or teaching during the pandemic?
Hard-Working History Teacher:

- We're going to see the effects of this pandemic for our students and teachers for a long, long time.
- Teaching is a tough job.

- I would not recommend it to as many people as I did when I first started.
- A pay increase would help as well as more respect from local school officials and people outside of teaching.
- I don't have a lot of energy to fight fires, but I do want my students to have a learning environment that is comfortable and conducive to learning. That is what I have tried to do as best as I can during this pandemic and will continue to do until my last day as a teacher.

My response:
Thank you for taking the time to answer my many questions with such care.

You've highlighted the good, bad, and ugly in one go.

Every batch of kids is different, but the current batch seems to have more that need to re-learn how to function in public than past years. That is likely a result of virtual and hybrid teaching due to the Covid-19 pandemic.

I hope the effects are shorter-lived than you've estimated.

And I hope you have a long and successful teaching career where you continue to touch the lives of many students.

Takeaways:
- Teaching can be tough.
- The pandemic threw education for a few loops the past few years.
- Kids and teachers rose to the occasion, but not as much learning took place for a variety of reasons.

Chapter 30:
Episode 90 – General Opinion: That's a Wrap – End of the School Year

Introduction:

Dear Reader,

For large portions of the population, change is not a comfortable thing.

It can be exciting or scary or something in between.

Throughout the series, we've discussed some of the ways that teaching differs from many other professions.

One of the most misunderstood times of year is the summer.

What do teachers do over the summer?

Note: Some schools have moved to an all-year schedule, so they get smaller breaks more often rather than a true summer. The things discussed here may still apply because there's still a sense of promoting the students to a new level.

~Ann

To get paid or not to get paid.

Most teachers are ten-month employees.

Most schools offer an option for ten-month employees to get paid throughout the summer. That means, their salary is split so they get paid over the course of twelve months. This also means that the paychecks are smaller accordingly.

My school does not have an option for being paid over the summer, and I doubt this is unique to my district. Even though my sample size was very small, many people indicated they do get paid throughout the summer.

Not getting paid in the summer is fine for me. I find plenty to do, but it does require some people to be much better at budgeting.

Teacher reactions to the end of a school year:
- Tears of joy (probably some of relief mixed in there)
- Tears of sadness
- A feeling of relief
- Mental switching of gears over to a new year

Why tears of joy or a sense of relief?
- Teaching can be stressful, so having that end for a time can make one giddy.
- There's a sense of pride in sending a batch of students on to the next level.
- The switch over to summer usually heralds good things like more time with family.

Why tears of sadness?
Every class is different. Every kid is different.

Teachers spend a lot of time around students, especially in the lower grades where the primary teacher is responsible for most of the subjects. Emotional attachments are bound to be made.

Why is there a mental switch?

Some people have to mentally gear up to get ready to welcome a new class. You need to make peace with not seeing some of the kids and emotionally recover both from ones that ripped your heart out and ones you'd like to never meet in this life again.

Elementary teachers have to plan themes and room decorations.

I think to some extent everybody makes some shift, but it's more extensive in some cases. To some, if they do not get that chance to flip, they have a difficult time settling into a new year.

I suppose that's an argument for having a true summer. I'm not sure two to three weeks would be enough for certain teachers to make that mental change.

Seasons aside:

In a traditional school, every school year progresses through seasons.

- Beginning of school – Kind of a honeymoon stage with the kids.
- Middle of the first quarter – By now, most teachers know the names and personalities of the students.
- End of the first quarter – Mad scramble for some kids to pass. You get a beat on who's going to struggle.
- Beginning of the second quarter – Usually getting to the heart of the content. Fall state testing extravaganza.
- Middle of the second quarter – Several holiday interruptions.
- Third quarter – Some long stretches without a break.
- Fourth quarter – Spring sports, prom season for high schools, Spring state testing extravaganza, and the great winddown and everything that goes along with that.

Quite a few seasons involve the students turning into distractable crazy people.

Admission: Okay, so a few seasons also involve the teachers being at the so-done-with-this-junk point too.

What do teachers do over the summer?
Make money stuff:
- Tutor
- Get a part-time job
- Teach summer school
- Work at summer camps
- Concentrate more on their side hustle

Side hustle (lucrative hobbies) aside:
I suppose anything that makes one money that isn't related to teaching could be considered a side hustle.

I've heard of everything from selling candles to being a DJ as a side hustle. By the broadest definition, writing is my side hustle.

From a certain point of view, it's a hobby that makes one money, but in many ways, it's also a second job.

I tend to do a lot of writing over the summer.

Work stuff:
- Attend school-related conferences
- Prepare for the new school year – One can never be too prepared.
- Do professional development (conferences, online programs, etc.)
- Further personal education by taking courses toward a master's degree or a doctorate.

Fun stuff:
- Rest
- Hike
- Write

- Swim
- Camp
- Go on vacation
- Go to the beach
- Summer concerts
- Take classes for fun
- Read/listen to audiobooks
- Attend non-school related conferences
- Take care of their kids/spend extra time with their kids

Most people do some combination thereof.

Takeaways:
- Summer looks different to teachers.
- Having a break is a chance to recharge.
- Some people have to work over the summer because bills don't stop but the paycheck might depending on the school district.

Chapter 31:
Episode 91 – Special Guest: Creative Art Teacher Part 1 – Background

Introduction:

Dear Reader,

There are several things that will make you feel old as a teacher.

One is seeing former students all grown up and having babies. (Check. Thanks, social media.)

Two is talking to your former teachers as a colleague or as a professional peer. (Also, check.)

Third is teaching one of your former student's kids. (I haven't reached that status yet—thank goodness.)

The fourth is having one of your former students become a teacher and then talking to them about their job. (We are here!)

Please join me in extending a warm welcome to Creative Art Teacher.

Feeling kind of old here,

~Ann

How many years have you been teaching?
Creative Art Teacher: Two officially, since becoming certified. However, I taught at a homeschooling co-op group for two years, and then, worked as a substitute teacher for five years prior to getting my certification. I guess you could say nine years if you include those experiences.

Me: Yes, those definitely count.

Fun fact (from me): I wasn't a state certified teacher for the subject when I had you as a student. (I had a state certification for a different subject.)

Private schools don't require it. They simply have to trust you know the subject well enough and are willing to put in the time, energy, and effort to prepare lesson plans to their specifications.

Did you have a different career?
Creative Art Teacher: No, but I had many part-time jobs between when I started my college education in 2012 and when I graduated in 2020.

Did you have friends in high school?
Creative Art Teacher: Yes, but I wouldn't consider myself popular then or now.

Me: General popularity can be overrated. Most people will develop a few deep friendships, but even those can come and go with seasons of life.

Did you get close to any teachers when you were a student?
Creative Art Teacher: Yes, I had a few teachers I feel I was close to: my junior year English teacher and my senior year art teacher.

Fun fact: I worked with my high school art teacher's husband during my student teaching internship, so I was able to reconnect with my old art teacher through that.

Me: See, this is why mothers tell kids to behave everywhere. It's a very small world.

Why did you choose teaching as a career?
Creative Art Teacher: I have always had a passion for art. I also had many wonderful art teachers from my time in grade school and college.

However, it was during my second year of college when I had the opportunity to work as a volunteer art teacher at a homeschooling co-op that convinced me.

From my first day, I fell in love with teaching.

I loved how I could couple my passion for art, with helping children and teenagers build their artistic skills and grow in their creativity.

I still love getting to see that spark and enjoyment as my students learn new skills or find something that clicks for them in a new way, through my art classes.

How long does it take you to prepare a lesson for a class?
Creative Art Teacher: For the start of a new art project, it takes a few hours collectively (per class).

I'd say eight to ten hours per project, with a new project every two to three weeks.

I teach three different art courses at my school, so I just try not to start a new project in all of my classes at the same time (for my own sanity, haha).

Me: Probably for the best, though who knows, that might lead to heightened creativity.

What do you consider prep for a class and how do you approach it?

Creative Art Teacher: For me, prep involves writing the lesson plan and establishing learning objectives connected to the curriculum, as well as creating a variety of things such as:

- project samples
- demonstration videos
- learning aides
- technique sheets
- rubrics

And preparing materials for the students to do the project. This involves things like cutting paper.

Some of my prep work is done at school, but some of it, such as creating the project samples and videos, is done at home, so I have the technology to do what needs to be done.

What kind of school do you work in?

Creative Art Teacher: I have taught at a Catholic high school, but last school year, I taught at a public school (elementary level).

Which classes did/do you teach?

Creative Art Teacher: I teach Art 1, Art 2, and Graphic Design. Next year, I will also be teaching an AP Art course.

What's the most preps you've had in a year?

Creative Art Teacher: Both this school year and last, I had one class period per day that I could use as a prep period.

However, last school year (working as an elementary art teacher), I had significantly more classes and students to prepare for, as I had about 750-800 students I taught per week.

(**Translation:** That's like 150-160 students per day!)

This year, I have about 120 students, and I see each class every day.

Me: Ha, well, I guess there is a third meaning for the word prep. I meant it as in separate types of classes you taught. From your answer, I gather that the answer might be next year and four preps (types of classes).

Definition three: A prep is a period a teacher gets off in which to complete the preparation for a class.

Also, I think my soul just died a little at the idea of having 800 students in a week.

I think the most I've ever had in a year was up around 90 to 100 per class, so about 500 if we're counting by week.

Takeaways:
- Art teachers tend to teach a lot of courses.
- Art teachers have a lot of students in many of their classes, especially the general ones.
- I never considered the physical project prep as part of my preparation time, but it certainly counts.

Chapter 32:
Episode 92 – Special Guest: Creative Art Teacher Part 2 – Reactions and Takeaways

Introduction:
Dear Reader,

Art comes in many forms.

Some people make a whole career out of indulging in creative projects and teaching others the wonders of doing so.

My stick figures are ugly, and I haven't the patience to paint something that isn't toddler style finger paint. But I admire those who can do classic art well.

~Ann

What is your favorite class to teach?
Creative Art Teacher: My favorite classes to teach this year are Art 1 and Art 2.

What is your favorite topic to teach?
Creative Art Teacher: Hard to say.
- Maybe the color theory?
- Acrylic painting unit?
- Or possibly the shading and drawing of three-dimensional forms?
- Or possibly printmaking?

Me: I can tell you love what you do. I should probably learn more about color theory. The closest I come to visual arts is describing what I'd like my cover to look like to one of the two artists I turn to consistently.

What is your least favorite class to teach? Why is it your least favorite?
Creative Art Teacher: Graphic Design.

I am more proficient with working with my hands than digitally to create a work of art that matches my original vision.

I was also learning the Adobe suite of programs right alongside my students this year.

Me: I've seen Adobe. It's awesome and very scary. So many buttons.

When do you think the emphasis on grades kicks in for students?
Creative Art Teacher: (When in general?)
I would say middle school for most kids, but if not then, definitely high school. The importance/emphasis on grades can begin younger depending on expectations at home.

(When, as far as within my own subject matter?)
I would say some kids have an excellent work ethic and enjoy learning and growing in their creativity (regardless of their skill level) and for them, the work they create in the art room is a reward

in itself and the grades just follow naturally.

(I should note that I focus more on effort, work ethic, and an attempt at the skills learned, especially in my introductory classes, than on the final product alone).

However, for some students, if there isn't a grade attached to an assignment, they won't make the effort because they just don't care. Once they see zeros in the gradebook for not doing an assignment, then they (usually) care.

Every project I give, every homework assignment or technique sheet, has a grade attached to it to (hopefully) keep all students on track and working.

While art is fun, I take my subject seriously and always remind students of the importance of art, visual communication, and creative expression, and I feel that grades help to maintain that serious attitude.

Me: That might be the most thorough, lovely answer I've gotten to that question to date.

What is the best, worst, and most fun part of teaching for you?
Creative Art Teacher:
Best:

- The best part of teaching is developing relationships with students and seeing them grow in their skills, knowledge, and character.
- I love hearing from students that they haven't painted or used pastels or done another art-related activity since elementary or middle school, and they forgot how enjoyable it was.

Worst:

- The worst part is the inattention (due primarily to cellphones) and the behavior issues.
- While many/most of my students are well-behaved, I have some students that are downright disrespectful (as all teachers have).
- Also, due to the current sociopolitical climate of our country, there are some students that assume a white teacher like me is "racist" when I have to correct or discipline a student of color, or if such students don't earn a perfect score (Never mind the fact that I have students of all ethnicities that I need to correct from time to time, or who don't receive a good grade on an assignment and all augments are graded using a rubric for consistency and clarity).

Me: Cellphones in classrooms are a nuisance. Maybe try starting off with a cellphones-stay-in-backpacks rule next year. Won't be perfect, but it may cut down on the amount of wasted breath you spend on yelling about phones.

School policies on this vary but are usually trash because the school doesn't want to look bad to the parents.

That's sad about the random racism accusations. I should write a chapter about that. I've heard it happen within my class. Mostly boys being mean (and dumb) to their friends.

I want to say it's mostly kids just being idiotic, but I think society as a whole has trained them to cry racism at anything and everything, which is totally not going to help solve the real issues.

Most fun:

- I would say the most fun part of my job is sharing my passion for art with students of all skill and interest levels.

- I also love getting to know all of my students and laughing with them and enjoying their sense of humor and creativity.

Are you involved in any extracurriculars as a teacher?

Creative Art Teacher: I lead two after-school clubs, the Art Club and the Charity Ornament Club (students make and sell Christmas ornaments using the school laser cutter and donate all profit to a charity of the school's choosing).

Me: I've never heard of such a club (Charity Ornament Club), but it's a great idea.

Do you have any advice for new teachers?

Creative Art Teacher:

- Don't lose your passion or your ability to connect with and relate to your students.
- While fashion trends and popular music will change, and technology is ever-evolving, at the end of the day, your students are still kids. They need empathy, kindness, structure, and a caring and knowledgeable teacher.
- Also, be more firm at the start of the school year. It is easier to *loosen up* as the year goes on, than do damage control and try to be firmer as the school year progresses.

Me: All great thoughts. I especially love the first one.

How did the pandemic affect teaching for you?

Creative Art Teacher: For me, I'm thankful I did my student teaching before the pandemic, in a classroom that had great technology and a cooperating teacher that employed a flipped classroom method with demonstration videos.

This gave me the practice I needed to teach in virtual and hybrid formats, without sacrificing the quality of an arts education.

While I was successful in this regard, this is only a part of the puzzle, and most teachers struggled to figure out the necessary switch to technology.

- In addition, students have gaps in their knowledge in all subject areas, as well as social gaps. In many ways, students are less mature and less focused than prior to the pandemic.
- I would venture to say these gaps are even more pronounced in younger, elementary-aged students.

My response:
I like your distinction between academic and social gaps.
It's been a pleasure speaking with you. May you continue to bring a love of art to students for many years. Best of luck with your future classes.

Takeaways (What do you think kids need to succeed at school?)
Creative Art Teacher:

- Students need caring teachers who are experts in their subject matter.
- I think that parental involvement and a group of friends who are a positive influence also set students up for success.

Chapter 33:
Episode 93 – Second Veteran Homeschooler Part 1 – Why I Choose Homeschooling

Introduction:

Dear Reader,

School choice has been a hot topic over the years. Everybody wants to know that their kids get the best education in a safe environment.

Homeschooling is a fascinating and flexible option for those who have the means to do it.

It's not an option for everybody, but it's always interesting to hear individual stories.

I recently had the chance to talk with another Veteran Homeschooler (mom).

Let's hear from her.

~Ann

What would you like me to call you?

A name? I haven't a clue! I guess you can pick something if you'd like.

Me: Great. I shall call you Second Veteran Homeschooler. That's short for Second Veteran Homeschooler to Tolerate My Many Questions.

Did you have a job before becoming a homeschooler?

Second Veteran Homeschooler: I've been homeschooling for nine years since my oldest child was in kindergarten.

Before my two kiddos were born, I was a travel agent. I owned my own business which was something I really loved doing.

But it wasn't being a mom or an author, and really, that was where my heart was.

Me: Guess you have two jobs now. Glad you get to live out your dream jobs. Writing is particularly good as a side job because it gives one the ability to escape to a different world for a time.

Were you homeschooled?

Second Veteran Homeschooler: No, I attended traditional brick and mortar schools.

Did you get close to any teachers when you were a student?

Second Veteran Homeschooler: One when I was a junior in HS.

Did you enjoy school as a kid?

Second Veteran Homeschooler: No, not really. We moved a lot so the friends I made I would have to leave again.

Me: That's hard. I wonder if it would be different in the current day and age with the internet and cell phones and such. Connecting with people is simultaneously harder and easier, but it might have let you keep some of those friendships through frequent moves.

Why did you choose to homeschool your children as opposed to other types of schools?

Second Veteran Homeschooler: Because of the violence in schools now.

The school shootings were a major player in the decision—the idea of not being able to send my kiddos to school and know they were safe. I also didn't like the way school funding was going.

Me: I'm sure that's a concern that weighs on a lot of hearts and minds.

What do you mean by "the way school funding was going"?

Second Veteran Homeschooler: Schools don't have the resources they once had.

Teachers are having to spend their checks on getting supplies for the classroom and still programs are cut for the kids.

We have the flexibility to do things the way we want to do them without having to worry about those issues.

Me: My school provides some supplies. I do end up buying my own stuff though. (Pencils. Lots of pencils.) There's definite value in a quality pencil sharpener.

How did it work to register with your state?

Second Veteran Homeschooler: I'm trying to remember, it's been a while!

I think I just went online to the Parent Portal of K12, filled in the fields, and then waited for them to contact me. They need to verify residency, etc. so it's a whole process of getting together the correct documents.

At the time, there was a waiting list, but that went pretty quickly, we were accepted, and that was it.

Me: I find it odd that there was a waiting list for homeschool, but I suppose bureaucracy always has some wait times. And you were applying for a specific program.

What's the hardest part of running homeschool?
Second Veteran Homeschooler: Probably keeping the kiddos motivated and getting through the days when the kids don't feel like doing it, and they're home, so they feel like they don't have to try as hard (and that's harder when they're younger than it is now. They've gotten used to it and know school time is school time, no exceptions.)

What qualities do you have are applicable to making you a better homeschooler?
Second Veteran Homeschooler: Patience, the ability to adapt to the day and shift directions if something isn't working, a willingness to learn with them—all these things are key to homeschooling.

And honestly, some days are better than others. But it's a journey, and I think the biggest thing is to enjoy the journey with your children and never forget to be amazed by it.

Me: Even in traditional schools there are good days and days that could definitely go better. If you don't keep yourself grounded, you can easily get overwhelmed. I imagine that's true for homeschool situations as well.

Do you have a routine?
Second Veteran Homeschooler: Yes.

The homeschooling program we chose actually has online teachers that help with the process, and now that my oldest is in middle school, the online teachers have taken over her instruction nearly 100% so we have to go by their schedule.
Me: Interesting. So, it's a form of virtual schooling.

How did you choose that program? What curriculum do you use?

Second Veteran Homeschooler: We heard about it when my oldest was born and I did some research.

We liked the program K12 has, the fact that they are nationwide, so if we ever relocated (which we did) we could take the school with us and fall within each state's laws and regulations for homeschooling, and the fact that as they grew into more advanced subjects (think math here—NOT my strong suit), the teachers would teach them.

Me: Math starts out all innocent and easy and then *wham* geometry and precalculus.

Do your kids to any organized sports or other extracurriculars?

Second Veteran Homeschooler: Right now, no. But they are becoming enrolled in an extra art school where all their art supplies are included, and we can work around their academic schedule to do that.

Me: That amount of flexibility is great.

That's about the time we have for today, but we'll pick up with this gracious guest next chapter.

Takeaways:
- One popular reason parents choose to homeschool their kids is the incidents of school violence.
- There are programs such as K12 that are essentially virtual schools where the students learn from home but get taught by certified teachers.
- Homeschooling schedules are highly flexible.

Chapter 34:
Episode 94 – Second Veteran Homeschooler Part 2 – Have Awesome Discussions

Introduction:

Dear Reader,

We're joined once again by Second Veteran Homeschooler.

Parents who homeschool probably learn a lot right alongside their kids.

While school can sometimes get bogged down in the state tests and individual assessments and finals, there's more to learning than that. In a way, emphasizing that part takes a lot of the joy out of learning.

Side note: Learning for learning's sake can be fun. I've had students who taught themselves how to speak Korean because it interested them.

I like that there are so many different ways to do homeschooling.

~Ann

What is your favorite subject/topic to teach?
Second Veteran Homeschooler: English and History

I guess if I had to pick one, I'd say History because while I love teaching English, the mechanical side of it can get boring for them. With History, we really look for stories and use Google Maps street view and try to make it come alive for them.

I also encourage my kids to understand there's never one point of view when it comes to history and at least two sides to everything. We don't have to agree with both sides, but to understand them can help understand why what happened took place. We've had some of our best discussions with history.

Me: I kind of liked diagraming sentences. Not sure they do that anymore since that's a skill that happens way before the level I teach at.

What is the best, worst, and most fun part of teaching?
Second Veteran Homeschooler:
- The worst thing is when they're not getting it, and you can't think of a way to come from another angle so that they can. It can be frustrating for them, and frustrating for you as a homeschool teacher and those are the moments where we all take a break and come back later.
- The best part, and the flipside of the worst, is when they do get it. You are there for every lightbulb moment and that is the greatest thing—to see your kids get it.
- The most fun is having those discussions; when we can make school more than reading a book or doing a worksheet.

Me: The ah-ha moment is universally a very popular part of any form of teaching. I suppose this is true concerning any sort of communication. It's frustrating when the audience misses the message.

The flipside is also true. It's highly satisfying when a message gets received and understood.

Worksheets have their uses. Books are amazing, but discussions are also vital to the learning process for some people.

What do you think kids need to succeed at school?

Second Veteran Homeschooler: I think they need to be taught in the style that works best for them. They all can learn the same material, but some learn it one way, some another.

Me: Traditional schools tend to cater to audio and visual learners. Sciences are also conducive to hands-on learning by way of labs.

How do you handle getting your kids around other kids (socialization)?

Second Veteran Homeschooler: We're lucky enough to live in a great neighborhood where they have friends that they can hang out with after school.

My youngest also met another girl in her class that lives nearby, and they've become best friends so that's really cool.

Me: Having friends certainly makes life interesting.

Do you have any advice for people considering homeschooling as an option?

Second Veteran Homeschooler:
- Do your research and find the option that works best for your family and your children.
- This is a personal journey for the entire family and don't be afraid to make it one.

- And don't listen to everyone outside your family when they say, "Don't do it!"
- If it's right for you, then do it, no regrets.
- Finally, be patient. Good days and bad days will come, and it's ok to adjust accordingly. (Sometimes, the internet won't work. Sometimes, the kids won't feel like working. Sometimes, you won't feel like working. Don't be afraid to let those moments come and react accordingly. Step away, and don't worry. School will still be there tomorrow.)

Me: Homeschoolers do move through their curriculums quickly. I guess that last piece of advice you need to take to heart in your situation. There's great value in the occasional mental health day. If it turns into mental health year, that might be a problem.

Takeaways and random other comments:
- School will be there tomorrow. – Agreed, but it may not always look the same. I'm sure everybody remembers March of 2020 when the Covid craze reached America. Schools—and a lot of things—changed overnight.
- Flexibility is one of the high points of homeschooling. Don't hesitate to use that to your advantage.
- One of the other homeschool parents mentioned that they like to take the kids on trips. Everything becomes a learning experience.
- Traditional schools are a relatively modern human concept. I'm a fan of traditional schools, but as this mother pointed out, not every kid learns the same way. For some, homeschool is the best option.
- Friends are valuable. Kids thrive when they can connect with peers.

Chapter 35:
Episode 95 – Special Guest: Classroom Parent Helper

Introduction:

Dear Reader,

I recently learned that some elementary classrooms and nursery schools have parent helpers.

It makes sense. It's just not something that crossed my mind, but I've been on the hunt for anything and everything related to education, which is how I stumbled across this concept.

I knew parents helped out with things like field trips because I'm pretty sure my mother went on some trips when I was in elementary school.

~Ann

Dear Ann,

When my son was in kindergarten, his school had opportunities for parents to be classroom helpers.

I was at the school every morning, and I walked my son to his classroom.

I don't remember exactly how I got involved, just that I filled out the background check forms so I could.

I usually arranged for my parent helper day to be on my sister's day off so she could babysit my toddler.

One morning, the teacher asked me if I could fill in for another parent who couldn't make it. Toddler welcome. So, my toddler and I were helpers that day.

(We helped prepare a craft that day.) We also got to help together a few more times.

One of the reasons I got involved was because I wanted to be involved. It was a very small school and I liked it a lot.

~ Classroom Parent Helper

Me: That's wonderful. I'm glad you got the opportunity. I have so many questions.

First, what made you want to be a classroom helper?
Classroom Parent Helper: I do think that parents should be involved with their kids, and this was just one way to do that.

What kind of school was it? (public or private?)
Classroom Parent Helper: It was a public school.

What were your duties in the classroom?
Classroom Parent Helper: As a parent helper, I got to help pass out snacks, help make sure hands were washed, help kids wipe down tables, prepare crafts, and even go on a field trip.

It was pretty simple things that helped keep the classroom running so that the teacher could concentrate on the bigger tasks.

The teacher I worked with had this motto, her job was to keep the kids safe. Their job was to help keep it that way.

I see being a parent helper was my way of making that possible.

What were the benefits of being a class helper?
Classroom Parent Helper: I felt like it helped to know my son's classmates.

How many parent helpers did the teacher have in a given year?
Classroom Parent Helper: The school was very small, so under 500 students.

I don't know how many parent helpers there were, but I know two other moms helped with the Christmas preparations.

It might have been like one helper a week. We did half-day kindergarten. It might have been more or less for other classes.

Did you have a favorite part of the experience?
Classroom Parent Helper: I just remember loving it, and when my three-year-old got to help too, that was awesome.

Me: Sounds like a great experience for your three-year-old.

Would you do it again if you had the chance?
Classroom Parent Helper: I would do it again, for sure.

What would you say to someone who was on the fence about becoming a class helper?
Classroom Parent Helper: If someone was on the fence about it, I'd say go ahead and give it a try. Maybe you'll get to decorate a bulletin board or hand out snacks. But it's a good memory and the time goes so fast.

Me: Thanks for sharing that wonderful experience.

Because I got curious, I threw *parent helper* into Google, just to see what it had to say. As usual, it came through with 136 million hits.

The first site was from a nursery school.

Highlights were much the same as our guest described. I imagine a kindergarten class has most of the same responsibilities.
- Cleanup duties
- Snack duties
- Play duties

I think it just helps to have another adult present to help watch the tiny humans.

One benefit that might not have been highlighted but is worth mentioning is that it's nice to be able to foster a good relationship with your child's teacher.

Relationships are two-way things. Teachers often strive to reach out to parents to say positive things and connect on potential problems. Helping can head off some tension before it builds.

Takeaways:
- If you get the chance to help in your child's classroom, go for it. There are great memories to be made.
- It may seem like menial tasks, but each one facilitates the smooth running of the classroom. When you get to high school, the students are capable of cleaning up after themselves in case of water spills and such. (Whether they choose to do so is another matter.)
- Some of the lower grades just need that extra pair of helping hands.

Chapter 36:
Episode 96 – Special Guest: Adjusting Empty Nester

Introduction:

Dear Reader,

The end of the school year brings many things, including rising-next graders, preschoolers ready for the official kindergarten, highschoolers headed off to trade schools and colleges, and a new batch of parents sending their kiddos into the world.

Time flies. It's something I tell many of my students every year. On my quest to get parents to weigh in, I decided to ask them more specifically about transitions. Several lovely people graciously shared their experiences.

Here is the first of them.

~Ann

Hi. What would you like me to call you?

Adjusting Empty Nester

Sounds good. Please share a bit about your family and school background.

Adjusting Empty Nester: I have two kids who passed through the public school system. The younger one, who is 19, just finished his freshman year in college.

Me: That's a big step.

What is your current situation? Or What was the last milestone your child passed?

Adjusting Empty Nester: Last milestone was graduation from high school.

Why did you choose the schools your kids attended?

Adjusting Empty Nester: Didn't choose. My kids attended their local public schools.

Which was the hardest transition for you?

Adjusting Empty Nester: For me? Graduating high school and going off to college. Probably the hardest for my kid too!

There was also a little sadness when my second kid went from elementary to middle school. We had a close connection to our local elementary school as it was just down the street, and I often went in and volunteered at parties, school trips, etc.

We never had the same kind of connection to middle and high school.

Which was the easiest transition for you?

Adjusting Empty Nester: Easiest was probably middle school to high school.

Did your child do the typical high school rites of passage?

Adjusting Empty Nester: Nope! My son's a math and choir nerd! He chose, very vocally, NOT to attend dances, proms, sports games, etc. He was in show choir though and is still in choir in college.

How involved with your kids' schooling were you?
Adjusting Empty Nester: I'm a strong believer in letting my kids make their own mistakes.

And a guilty secret: I HATED the kind of parent homework that we were forced to do in preschool and elementary school. I remember right in kindergarten for the 100th day of school they asked the kids (but really the parents) to create a 100-day project.

The mother down the street sewed A HUNDRED buttons onto a hat for her daughter!!! NO, NO, NO!! I was never going to do anything like that. I gave my daughter a piece of construction paper and a bucket of stickers and told her to count out 100 of them and stick them on the paper and that was her project that she did herself!

My son, three years later, actually came up with his own 100-day project—a chart of Roman Numerals in little windows from 1 to 100 that he made entirely by himself.

(Can you tell he's a math major?)

As the kids grew older, me and my husband were always available when they had questions, but on the whole, we stayed out of their school stuff other than just nudging them occasionally to finish their homework.

Me: That 100-day project sounds interesting and a little horrifying for parents. I'm pretty sure some parents do kids' projects up through high school.

Side note: One of my friends was just complaining that his elementary-aged kid had to bring in a cake in the shape of our state. Yeah, that's not exactly a kid-appropriate project.

Did your child receive any special services?
Adjusting Empty Nester: My son had speech in early elementary school.

What do you think was the most valuable experience of high school?
Adjusting Empty Nester: My son had an odd high school experience as a year and a half of his time was eaten by COVID. But as an introvert he didn't really suffer from virtual school in the same way as some of his schoolmates. He forged good relationships with his teachers, particularly in math and science and that has led to his success so far in college.

Me: I'm glad he fared well with the crazy changes. It seems that most didn't adjust well, but there was always 1-2 kids per class who absolutely thrived in the virtual school environment.

What was the college application process like?
Adjusting Empty Nester: Odd (because of COVID). My son only ended up applying to three colleges, all of which accepted him and offered him scholarships. He did toy with taking a gap year because of the virus and would have done so had the vaccinations not been available in time.

Me: Congrats to him. That's a great accomplishment.

I only applied to three when I was in high school, but these days, I see stacks of like eight to ten in the recommendation portal.

Did you visit colleges?
Adjusting Empty Nester: We visited a couple before COVID, but our main trip was supposed to be in Spring Break of his Junior year at high school and that was cancelled because of the virus. He ended up visiting virtually and choosing UWM in Milwaukee without ever having visiting it!

If you could do it over again, would you change anything?
Adjusting Empty Nester: Not really.

What advice do you have for parents in your situation?
Adjusting Empty Nester: Let your kids lead!

An awful lot of parents I see push their kids towards colleges and fields of study that they feel are worthwhile. While you do have some say if you're paying, it should ultimately be your kid's choice.

Other closing thoughts?
Adjusting Empty Nester: Enjoy your time with your children. It's all over in a heartbeat!

Being an empty nester is odd and a little sad, but technology means that I'm still able to check in with my son most days even if it's only to share Wordle scores.

Me: That's an excellent reminder. Thanks for stopping by and sharing that with us.

Takeaways:
- Support your kids through their school, but don't do their work for them.
- Guide your kids, but also, give them room to grow and become the people they want to be.
- Enjoy every moment you get with your kids. Time goes quickly.

Chapter 37:
Episode 97 – Special Guest: Super Mom (Special Needs and Pre-K Parent)

Introduction:

Dear Reader,

I find it fascinating to hear from people in different life situations. Our last guest is a recent empty nester.

Our new guest is just starting to help her kids navigate the school systems.

School dominates such a large portion of our lives. (Those who become teachers spend the majority of their lives haunting school halls.)

No matter which form education takes place in (public, private, virtual, home, boarding, or something else) it is the setting for some of our finest firsts, greatest accomplishments, and hardest lessons.

~Ann

What would you like me to call you?

Pre-k and special needs parent, maybe. I haven't had my coffee yet, I won't be able to think of anything witty.

Me: Let's go with Super Mom—that's short for Special Needs and Pre-K Kid Parent.

What's your family situation? Where are your kids on their school journey?

Super Mom:

- I went to school all over the place, in my younger years it was near the Catskills in New York.
- I have two children with my husband.
- The children are five and three.
- The five-year-old is graduating pre-k, and the three-year-old is entering into a special needs school in the fall. (She is currently in therapy for speech and cognitive skills.)
- Both are girls and so smart.

What is your current schooling and life situation?

Super Mom: I am in nursing school, and a writer as well as a homemaker.

- I am constantly with my children, and they have both reached milestones splendidly.
- My five-year-old is graduating pre-k and entering kindergarten knowing how to spell and read a few words and has a great grasp on the English language.
- My three-year-old has finally started to say her first words in the last few months (from therapy).
- She has been diagnosed with autism, and I am so proud of her for everything she has done.

Me: Sounds like you have more than enough to keep you busy. I've heard nursing school is pretty intense.

What was the application process for nursing school like?

Super Mom: The nursing application is easy, but you have to complete a set of prerequisites before applying, and that is where I am.

Me: Good luck. Nursing is a noble but exhausting career, though I suppose the same could be said for being a mother too.

Why did you choose the schools your kids attended?

Super Mom: I chose the school, because my three-year-old's program offered pre-k, and it was easier for me to go to one or two (depending on the day) places instead of three. Also, it helps my five-year-old to be introduced to others with ADHD and autism like her sister.

Me: It's nice to be around a variety of people.

Which was the hardest transition for you?

Super Mom: I would say the transition from home to school, in getting the girls and myself motivated to find a morning routine that didn't create a migraine.

Me: I only have to motivate me, and that can be a challenge some days. I guess people gain whatever skills they need as necessary. Glad you found your less painful routine.

Which was the easiest transition for you?

Super Mom: Sometimes with the overlap of school and classes for the girls, I end up with an hour to myself. That was pretty easy to enjoy.

Me: Me time can be very powerful.

How involved with your kids' schooling are you?

Super Mom: I go to every function and therapy class. I feel I am very involved.

If you could do it over again, would you change anything?

Super Mom: Not much. Things fell into place well, and everything I got was from finding a case worker for my three-year-old's needs. The case worker did amazing things for me and made my life easier.

Me (note to self): I should really talk to a special needs case worker someday.

What advice do you have for parents?

Super Mom:

- Take it one day at a time.
- Go through your county for services, and they will most likely provide them free.
- Everything is an accomplishment, even something so small as writing their name or saying their first words.
- It's okay to be frustrated, and very natural when starting the school life with your kids.
- Make friends with other parents in the same situation.

Me: Great advice. Networking is an excellent idea in most situations.

Takeaways:

- Every kid is unique.
- Accomplishments don't have to be earth-shattering to be significant.
- Get your kids the best care and support right from the beginning.
- Most public school districts provide special needs services. (Some have a better reputation than others. This might be something to keep in mind when searching for a home since districts are mostly arranged by residency.)

People have gone through similar situations. When possible, tap into their wisdom and experience.

Chapter 38:
Episode 98 – Special Guest:
Music and Drama Teacher Part 1

Introduction:
Dear Reader,

Sometimes, the teacher chooses the career, and sometimes, the career chooses the teacher.

It sounds like the latter case might be in play for our latest guest.

~Ann

What would you like me to call you?
Ooh, I don't know, I'm not creative enough to come up with something!

Me: Then, I shall call you Music and Drama Teacher, even though we could add a dozen other class titles.

How many years have you been teaching?
Music and Drama Teacher: I just finished year #2.

Ann Y. Mouse

Did you have a different career?
Music and Drama Teacher: Before teaching, I worked at a variety of clerical sort of jobs while I pursued a career in musical theatre.

I guess it depends on if you count *pursuing an acting career* as a career. That's what I considered my career for five years (plus studying for that career while in college), but since I only infrequently got paid to act, I'm not sure everyone would count that as a *career*.

Me: Since you studied for that profession and got paid to do it at all, I'd say it counts.

Did you have friends in high school?
Music and Drama Teacher: I had two very close friends in high school. One of them was my childhood best friend. We went to elementary school together, then went to separate schools in middle school, and she transferred to my high school our sophomore year.

The other was a girl who was new to my school in 9th grade, and I was the person she shadowed on the first day of school to show her where everything was. We joked that we never "unshadowed" because we were friends from that point on.

Did you get close to any teachers when you were a student?
Music and Drama Teacher: When I was a scared, shy, new girl in 6th grade, one of my teachers really connected with me. She had super curly hair like I did so we bonded over that, and she was probably the teacher I got closest to. She left after my 7th grade year though, so I didn't have her very long.

Why did you choose teaching?
Music and Drama Teacher: Mostly because the opportunity presented itself.

Covid had completely shut down the theatre industry. And even before that, I was beginning to wonder if I should make theatre more a side pursuit and find another thing to be my actual *job*.

(I could see the theatre industry moving in a direction that included me less and less—edgier stories, more pop-inspired scores—and not much demand for this traditional, blonde, legit-soprano. I didn't want to struggle through doing material I didn't like in the hopes that I'd eventually become successful enough to get hired for stuff I like, when I can do stuff I like in high-quality community theatre.)

But when Covid hit, the decision sort of got made for me. Then the headmaster from the school my sister taught at called me out of the blue and asked if I'd be interested in teaching Music and Drama at the school.

I never intended to become a teacher, but I was wondering what direction my life/career should take and God placed that in front of me.

How long did it take you to prep for class?
Music and Drama Teacher: Before I started the job, I was in another state and didn't know my curriculum or what to do, so I couldn't really prep until I moved and talked with the curriculum director. By that point, I didn't really get much time to prep before school started.

As far as daily/weekly prep for class, it's hard to say. Too long, probably.

Me: Pretty sure the soul of every teacher ever just said *amen*.

Music and Drama Teacher: I'm a perfectionist, and I also am much more comfortable when on a script, so I try to plan out every little moment of every little class.

I used to write a script for myself, complete with all my transitional phrases so I wouldn't freeze up and not know what to say. I do that less now that I've had a little more classroom experience, but I think I still spend too long prepping.

It also depends on the class. Once we're mid-production in Drama class, I don't need to do a whole lot of prep for class, other than looking over the scheduled scenes and reviewing my notes from the previous rehearsal.

(There are TONS of outside work associated with mounting a production, but I don't count that as class prep.)

Then there were classes like Rhetoric where I wasn't very familiar with the subject, and I needed to first learn the material myself, talk to the teacher from the other section to make sure I understood it correctly, and do all the homework assignments myself so that I knew what to teach the kids.

That took longer.

Then with Art class, certain projects for the young ones required cutting out enormous numbers of little paper birds or sailboats or flowers or whatever the project called for. I had around 40 kids in the class so if they each needed three sailboats, that's 120 sailboats I was cutting out.

That took me ages, until someone suggested letting some parent volunteers do the cutting. Great idea!

Me: I recently got to talk to a parent volunteer (Chapter 95). Yes, that's a perfect job for them. I can sympathize. I prepare notecards for my students once a year and that involves a lot of folding and cutting.

How do you approach prep?
Music and Drama Teacher: I don't really have a system. It's more "Okay, there will be kids in my classroom on Monday. What am I going to say to them?" and I go from there.

What kind of school did you work in?

Music and Drama Teacher: Small K-12 private Classical Christian School.

What classes did you teach?

Music and Drama Teacher: This past year I basically taught all the Specials and Electives: Elementary Music, Art, Physical Education, and Library, Middle School PE and Computer, High School Drama, and 9th Grade Rhetoric.

Me: Wow. Pretty sure you have everybody beat for sheer number of preps. That's kind of crazy.

What was the most preps you had in a year?

Music and Drama Teacher: I assume this means how many separate classes with different material, so I guess 8? 10, if you count Art and Music separately, but I didn't reach those at the same time since they alternated every quarter.

I had trouble keeping track of all of my classes last year. I think there was only once I forgot about a class while lesson planning for the week.

Me: That's understandable. 8 is a crazy number.

We're out of time for the chapter, so I'll kick the favorites question over to the next one. Always a pleasure to speak with performing arts teachers.

Takeaways:
- There's no one way to become a teacher. Many paths lead into and out of the career.
- Apparently, there's no one way to prepare for classes either.

Small Christian school teachers where many, many hats. I've run into this concept before just never to this degree. (This is why there can be a high turnover rate for teachers.)

Chapter 39:
Episode 99 – Special Guest:
Music and Drama Teacher Part 2

Introduction:
Dear Reader,

Today, we'll welcome back Music and Drama Teacher so she can tell us about her favorites and give us her advice.

~Ann

What was your favorite class to teach?
Music and Drama Teacher: Music and Drama.

For one thing, those are my areas of knowledge and passion, so it's natural I get most excited about those. But I also love that in those subjects it is so easy to see the fruit of the instruction.

Watching a group of kids go from just a group of kids with scripts in their hands to actors who can confidently create characters onstage and share a story with an audience is really cool. (Or hearing the progression from the kids don't know the song, to they know it but don't sing it well, to they know it and sing it well.)

Me: Guess I should have seen that answer coming.

What was your favorite topic to teach?

Music and Drama Teacher: I'm not sure if I'm understanding the distinction exactly right, but my favorite topic is not exactly a topic, but a task.

I like preparing the kids for a performance (whether the elementary Music kids' concert or the Drama kids' show). I think it's because there's a very clear and easy-to-see point to doing what we're doing.

Some stuff you learn in class can be sort of like *why am I learning this*? It's easy to feel like the only point is just so that they can know the things and pass the test. But when it's prepping a performance, everything is very practical.

What was your least favorite class to teach?

Music and Drama Teacher: Elementary Physical Education. I never liked PE class as a kid, but I had to teach it because of the schedule.

The kids got wild whenever they got in the gym because that's where they had recess and I think they saw the gym as a cue for *fun time*.

It was so loud and echoey in there that it was impossible to give instructions without yelling. And kindergarten PE was the worst because they really weren't old enough to grasp the concept of a game with rules and would basically just run wild. And it was particularly hard to rein them in or motivate them because I didn't like what I was having to teach.

I also "taught" a study hall my first year teaching and that was awful. 25 kids with no specific task ("I don't have any homework!" "I want to do mine at home.") shut in a room together and told to sit still and be quiet.

It was a train wreck. I gave out several detentions a week in that class. And I didn't know what to do—I was a brand-new teacher with no classroom management tricks and no material to try to keep them engaged. All I could do was say "sit down and be quiet" over and over and over.

Me: Not that I'd wish you back into that position, but hopefully, your previous years of teaching have given you some of those classroom management tricks to rely upon.

What is the best and worst part of teaching?
Music and Drama Teacher:
- I think the best part is seeing the kids really take hold of their lessons and take ownership of the material. Seeing them apply an acting technique during rehearsal or hear them singing the songs I taught in music class in the hallways or listening to them having a serious conversation about something they learned in science or history. Seeing them grow and learn is exciting.
- The worst part is dealing with behavior issues. I can have plans that would be so interesting and fun if the kids could just close their mouths for two minutes and listen. Then when I have to keep stopping to correct them, I lose my train of thought, so I fumble around to find it again, which makes the lesson more boring, which makes them more inclined to act up.

Do you have any advice for new teachers?
Music and Drama Teacher: I still consider myself a pretty new teacher, so I don't really feel like I'm in any place to give advice. Something that I often forget is that parents can be a resource. They can volunteer to help with tasks like cutting art papers or supervising backstage during shows or talking to their children at home about their behavior in school.

So, I guess the advice is "Don't forget about parents. You can talk to them."

Me: One goal for this project is breaking down some of the us vs. them barriers that exist between teachers and parents.

What do you think kids need to succeed at school?

Music and Drama Teacher: To me (in my limited experience) it seems like "success" is largely determined by attitude.

The kids just need the willingness to try their best, not to simply do the bare minimum to get by or to think that school is all about playing with their friends and classes are just an impediment.

The ones who can be really invested in their classes and eager to understand will succeed even if they aren't the best at the subject or necessarily getting the best grades.

Were you involved in any extracurriculars as a teacher?

Music and Drama Teacher: I helped my sister coach volleyball for half of last year's season, but I injured my knee in the process and was on crutches for a month.

I also was responsible for after-school care for the first part of last year so I couldn't make it to many practices/games once the school year started. I hope to help coach this year—hopefully with no injuries.

When do you think the emphasis on grades kicks in?

Music and Drama Teacher: I only teach Specials, so I don't give regular grades for any of my elementary kids. They get "skills" grades for effort and following directions, though I know they get grades in their regular classes.

I do give grades for the upper-level electives, but I'm usually pretty chill with the grading on those classes because it's more about learning the skills than on the grades. Basically, show up, try your best, and do what you're supposed to do, and you'll probably get an A.

How did the pandemic affect teaching?

Music and Drama Teacher: For me, it didn't really do anything. I started teaching in August 2020, so I have no pre-pandemic teaching experience. And my school was really lax on any sort of restrictions.

- Last year, we did temperature checks in the morning.
- I wore a mask, but I was one of four or five people in the school who did.
- I had three online students that I made videos for.

That was it, really. I guess the only effect for me was making it more difficult to rein in noisy children because I was masked (and muffled) and they were not. But this year was totally normal.

Takeaways:

- Success is largely determined by attitude.
- Don't forget that parents can be a resource.
- Seeing kids take ownership of their learning is a definite high point of teaching.

Chapter 40:
Episode 100 – General Opinion: An Open Letter to Students

Introduction:

Dear Reader,

Everybody has their own way of connecting with students. These ways usually coincide with the teacher's (or coach's or other school staff member's) interests.

Some can talk baseball, football, and hockey stats. Others bond over video games. Others share a love of multi-colored hair or nail extensions.

I'm a writer, so I write.

This is another milestone chapter, so I thought it would be fitting to share some of the collective sentiments I've learned through my career and this project thus far.

~Ann

Dear Student,
This letter might not flow in the traditional sense because it's just

a collection of thoughts and mini-lessons gathered over time.

Phones are wonderful tools, but try not to let it control you like an addiction. Look up from them once in a while.

Your generation has to face things the previous ones did not. This is just the way of life. We dealt with things you don't have to deal with, and the generation before us did the same.

Be strong. Be courageous.

Don't fear to forge your own path, yet understand that what is presented as the norm has merits too.

It's okay to disagree with people.

Attitude goes a long way in getting your way. It's not exactly just the art of manipulation. (Manipulation would be turning on charm for the sole purpose of getting your way.) My point is always approach stuff with a good attitude, and it'll go better for you.

It's a natural human tendency to want to help someone you like and be reluctant to help someone who's been nothing but trouble, heartache, and pain.

You may think I'm being melodramatic here, but I can assure you that much thought goes into how to deal with problem situations as they arise.

Teachers don't often like the discipline aspect of the job, but it's necessary for order and the smooth running of a classroom.

There are different kinds of yelling. Although it's tempting to be self-conscious and think everything's about you, sometimes the teacher's loud because the room is loud, not because he or she is angry with you.

The blame game isn't helpful. Teachers are resources. Parents are resources. But the work itself comes down to you. Own your education, and it will carry you a lot farther than if you passively wait for something to happen.

Surround yourself with good people, be they friends, family, or trusted adults.

You are unique, even if you're a twin or a triplet or one of more. There's never been someone like you.

You don't have to do anything to earn your place in this world. That said, hard work will carry you far. Effort goes a long way. We'll get you there if you work with us, but we can't produce straight up Biblical miracles with your grades.

If we're allowed to, we will fail you if you've earned that. This is a reflection of your efforts in a class, not your worth as a person. We may label you as lazy or useless in a class, but that's your behavior, again, not the person.

Often, teachers are just the messengers.

Rules and regulations are set by the administration, the school district, the state government, and the federal government.

We don't hand out state tests like candy because we want to. We don't have a choice. Those who control the money (in public schools anyway) have said thou shalt give these blasted tests, so we do. Trust me, we'd much rather be teaching the subject we're passionate about.

We (most of us anyway) know lack of consequences can kill motivation. That's why we try to establish norms within our classroom mini-kingdoms.

Rules such as don't leave the room without permission don't exist to annoy you. They exist to preserve something. The something could be the teacher's sanity, your life, classroom order, or something else entirely.

Fire drills and security drills aren't our favorite things. They disrupt the flow.

You're probably appalled by the much-publicized violence in schools. We are too. There's no easy answer to why some people find the need for attention so strong they decide to be as destructive as possible.

We want you to feel safe, but you must want that too.

We know you get frustrated when you don't understand, but try not to just shut down.

Traditional school isn't everybody's thing, and that's okay. You may not be lined up for an academic scholarship, but everybody can still find a measure of success.

College isn't the only life path beyond high school. The trades offer good careers.

Social media is a fun diversion, but it can preserve drama longer than it needs to be saved. Be cautious in how much of yourself you share with the world. You don't need to look far for examples of *some people are creepy.*

Learning's not a passive thing. It requires an investment of time, energy, effort, and attention. When these things are lacking, you have a harder time absorbing lessons.

I've seen people say they're just *no good* at science, but when they get time to work independently or in small groups, they're on their phones or chatting aimlessly. That's not a skill problem. That's an effort problem.

Teachers love you, even if we don't ever get to say it out loud. Love can be shown in many ways. It's those little above and beyond things that may or may not be known to you.

(Paying for extra pencils because you can't find one for your life. Buying a pencil sharpener. Moving due dates to accommodate a crazy schedule. Offering allergy-free lollipops. Staying up late to make sure you have a key to a worksheet.)

Time and health are two very important resources at your disposal. Use them well.

Every part of the life journey will have ups and downs. Enjoy the ups and weather the downs with good coping mechanisms.

We live in a time and place when for the most part if you really want something, you can obtain that goal if you are willing to invest the right amount of time, energy, and effort.

Try your best, then don't worry. Life's short enough without spending half of it stressed.

~Ann

Chapter 41:
Episode 101 – Special Guest: Military Mom Part 1 – Meet the Family

Introduction:

Dear Reader,

Every life journey is different.

Some people never have kids, and others have multiple sets of them.

Our latest guest has had a lot of life experience with her husband and seven children. It's such an intriguing tale, I think it might take us a few chapters to unpack.

~Ann

What would you like me to call you?

Military Mom

Me: I feel like I should add Super in between those words (and in front of every mom), but I'm not one to ruin great alliteration.

Tell us about your background and your kids' schooling backgrounds.

Military Mom:

Short version: We are a military family. Hubby is retired from being twenty years of active duty and has been working for the government (for the army) for the last twenty-three years.

The oldest child went to four different high schools, the next went to three, the 3rd and 4th to two. The daughter went to high school, then we have our two adopted Chinese daughters who have been in the same school.

So, my experiences are not the normal or average parental experience.

Me: Excellent. Those are the best kind of stories to hear. Bring it on.

Military Mom:

Longer version: My husband and I have been married for forty-three years. He was an Army helicopter pilot for twenty years, then when he retired, he was a government contractor.

We've had five biological children then when our youngest was ten, we adopted our first Chinese daughter and two years later we adopted another little girl who was a special needs baby with a repaired heart problem.

There is a twenty-five-year difference between our oldest son and our youngest daughter. The ages as of today are the sons: 42, 40, 36, 31 and daughters: 29, 18, and 17.

It was important to my husband and me that the boys had a strong background of self, community and family.

I made sure the boys—and all my kids—knew how to cook, clean, and do basic sewing.

I never wanted a daughter-in-law to come to me and say, "Why can't he do this?"

I wanted to say, "It's not because he can't, he just doesn't want to."

Me: Ah, yes, those are very different conversations.

Military Mom: We didn't know that we'd ever have a daughter as I was told I should not get pregnant again because the last son almost killed me, but obviously I didn't listen.

The boys are all Eagle Scouts and to this day they are involved in their communities, schools, and family.

The girls are also involved in a lot of activities in and out of school but mostly family. Going to church on Sundays was also very important even when the kids threw a fit because they didn't like it, they went because they knew it was required.

When they hit eighteen, they had a choice to go and most of the time they went without complaining.

The oldest daughter was diagnosed with UC (ulcerative Colitis), and at the age of twenty, she had a surgery to remove her large intestines and now wears an ostomy bag, but it does not stop her from doing the things she likes to do such as biking, hiking, swimming, rock climbing, and running. She has a boyfriend of several years and is happy.

I have always been a stay-at-home mom, but at times, I did finishing work for a local needlework shop.

It wasn't bad being a stay-at-home mom when the first three boys were small, but as they got older, less and less moms wanted to stay home and most places we lived I would be the only stay-at-home mom on the block.

Me: Bet that made you the fun mom.

Military Mom: I was the mom who made the cookies and kids would come over after school just for the cookies. I didn't mind; in fact, I loved it.

The only thing about being married to a career army guy was the chance that the kids would grow up to follow in dad's footsteps, and three of them did as much. At one time I had the three boys deployed at the same time, one in Iraq, two in Afghanistan, and then my husband was sent over to Afghanistan for business at the same time.

Needless to say, I didn't sleep much during all that; I was consumed with worry.

Me: That does sound very stressful.

Military Mom: As far as schools went, we moved about twelve times, and the kids always went to the closest ones to the Army base we lived on. When we lived in Florida, the two older boys went to magnet schools and were bused about twenty-five minutes away.

There wasn't much of a choice as we could not afford to send them to private schools. The younger two boys went to the public elementary school down the block.

When we lived in Illinois, we were able to send the boys to a Catholic school, and they thrived while going there.

The older boy went to four different high schools, and it wasn't a huge problem until he had a girlfriend. Then, he fought us tooth and nail to stay behind. Life as a mom was really hard then, but we didn't back down. His attitude changed after the first week of school, and he found a new girlfriend.

When we lived in Alabama our family changed after the oldest graduated as his friends were also son number two's friends, and when they weren't there, son number two felt lost and found other kids with the bad habits like smoking and drugs.

He fell hard into that group of kids and even though we did everything we were supposed to do such as when we found him overdosing in his bed we took him to the hospital, sent him to rehab, and made him see a psychologist, nothing really helped.

For the longest time, we didn't think he'd ever turn around, but after he had three kids, he turned himself around and got back to family and a good job he's now a hard-working single dad of four.

What was it like sending seven kids through the school system?
Maybe being a military wife for forty-three years makes it easy for me, having met so many people and being a stay-at-home mom the whole time.

Kids have been my whole life.

With seven kids I have enough for a book, and you'd not believe most of it really happened. My life could be considered either a sitcom or a horror show depending on how you look at it.

Things changed dramatically from the oldest kid starting school and my last two. It's almost like two lifetimes different.

Me: That's a perfect stopping point. Thanks for sharing a bit about your family.

Takeaways:

- Every kid is different.
- Being a mom can be fun.
- Being a mom isn't always easy.

Even kids who lose their way for a while can find their way back to a good path.

Chapter 42:
Episode 102 – Special Guest: Military Mom Part 2 – Transitions

Introduction:

Dear Reader,

I wrote this one before dealing with student failure but decided to present the heavier topic first.

Let's talk about a thing many students catch as the year comes to a close.

I've never worked in a school that goes all year with intermittent smaller breaks, but I'm sure they have similar problems when it comes to the last part of the school term before the students get their promotions to a new grade.

I discussed motivation some in the last chapter, but the basic definition for this thing is a complete crash of internal student motivation to do anything school related.

While still something that needs to be dealt with, there's a lot more hope for dealing with senioritis than a student either about to fail or who has already failed a course for the year.

~Ann

Senioritis:

If I threw the term into a search engine, I'd probably get a fine definition, but I've seen it enough to give you an adequate picture of the issue.

Senioritis is a state of mind that creeps over some seniors that can result in poor attitudes and precipitous grade drops.

It's not confined to seniors, but they are the most prone to it. Juniors and Sophomores still have people to impress if they want to get into a decent college. Freshmen have a long way to go in their high school careers.

*While these are the American terms for grades 9-12, I'm sure other countries have comparable grades and similar problems as the students sense the end of the year.

Causes of senioritis (and things that could make it worse):
- Being accepted to a college
- Being very close to passing all courses for the year

Symptoms of senioritis:
- Lack of focus - this is not confined to senioritis
- Lack of motivation
- A so-done-with-school attitude

Is there a cure?

There is no surefire cure for senioritis. Fortunately, it is a temporary affliction with a natural end called Summer's arrival. However, there are ways to work with the stricken and mitigate the effects.

Note: Some of these take a lot of foresight and careful planning.

Second note: The kids get antsy when any break looms on the horizon. It's just worse when that break is Summer. These may be good things to consider regardless of student age.

Teacher treatment and handling of senioritis:

- Adjust the year's lessons so the hard-hitting, mentally taxing units come first.
- Educational yet entertaining movies – Some subjects are a lot easier to find movies that work with the subject matter. Something like Forensic Science has many options because it's a fascinating subject with many stories to tell.
- A serious conversation about responsibility – It may not sink in now, but odds are good somebody will remember it at some point in their future. People often need to hear something multiple times before it grips them.
- Field trips – The way our year is laid out, the weather is nicer, so assuming nothing inconvenient like a world-wide pandemic hits, there are a lot of opportunities to get the kids out of the classroom.
- Breaks and other deals – I have had some limited success with being clear that I have a set amount of material that needs to be covered, but if we can accomplish my goals, they can have the last 5-10 minutes to relax, chat, and play on the phone. It turns into pure phone time 90% of the time, but that's fine.
- Wrap-up projects – These are good for any age. I recommend leaving the presentation part open ended. When given a choice to make a mini-film, create a PowerPoint or Slides presentation, create a Children's book, or a traditional poster project, most kids go with the easiest option. Go with the flow.

Parent/guardian treatment and handling of senioritis:

Disclaimer: These are ideas and suggestions only. How you've raised your kid thus far will determine their effectiveness.

- External motivation – Okay, so it's a bribe. I call this the carrot approach. I recommend caution with this one, but in moderation, this-for-that is powerful motivation. Don't get too crazy with expensive gifts (cars, large sums of cash) or unattainable goals (all A's if your kid traditionally pulls low B and high C scores).
- A serious conversation about responsibility – This one has arguably low efficacy, but it's still a solid one to try.
- Take the phone away – This is the stick approach, but in a way, it's also a carrot. It just doesn't seem carrot-y. You'd be surprised how effective this method is. It works blooming miracles in small doses.

Takeaways:
- Senioritis hits mostly Seniors, but the other grades are not completely immune.
- Planning ahead can minimize the need for a straight-up daily battle for classroom control.
- Parents too have a role in teaching students about the responsibilities they bear.

Chapter 43:
Episode 103 – Special Guest: Military Mom Part 3 – Advice

Introduction:
Dear Reader,

In this chapter, we get to hear some of the advice that Military Mom has both for other military parents and in general.

~Ann

Do you have any advice for other military moms/dads on navigating school with multiple kiddos?
Military Mom: Always make your move and the switch to a new school an adventure. If the kids believe you're in for that adventure, then they'll believe it too.

Let's face it, school is scary even if it's the same school and it's a new school year. It's a new room, new teacher(s), and new friends. I don't think that's changed since I graduated from high school. Granted, some things have changed like you need an ID to get in the building, and you need to push a buzzer to have the door unlocked, and you're always on camera somewhere.

But new can be unnerving. Tensions get high, and your children can argue and complain. Just remember how you felt when you were the new person.

Me: From a teaching standpoint, every new year is a challenge to settle into as well. There are 78-100 new faces and names to learn or more, depending on what subjects you teach.

There are kids whose names you learn before you have them because they're a behavioral problem. Flip side, there are quiet kids you slowly get to learn over time who have razor-sharp wit or are deep thinkers.

In a way, kids are like an unlabeled box of chocolates. You sometimes need to work at getting what's in their hearts.

How important is family and shared experience?
Military Mom: Family is the strongest support to have on your side be it by blood or by others in the same boat.

That's the best part of being in the military, you can always find someone else going through the same thing as you.

Take advantage of that and let your kids see you make new friends. Get them involved in something right away be it a sport, babysitting, band, or Scouts. Keep them enthused with whatever you or the child wants to start.

Be a part of the activity instead of dropping them off and leaving. Take the kids to the school before the school starts, take a tour, meet the teachers, and see the new classrooms.

Ask questions. Have the kids ask the new teachers questions. Have them write a list of questions to ask because we all know that you might have a great list of questions, but once you start speaking to that new person you all of a sudden forget most of those great questions.

I always took all the kids to see each classroom and teacher so they all knew where the other had to be and what the teacher looked like even if they forgot the teacher's name.

What other advice do you have for parents in general?

Military Mom: Advice? I just know what worked for us and may not work for anyone else.

I would say:

- Support your kid. Be there for your kid.
- Be patient 'cause being a kid today is really hard. It's not like when we were in school.
- Put them in Scouts or something like that.
- Let them make some decisions about what sport they want to do, not a sport you want them to do because you love doing it.
- If they need a parent for a field trip, go with them.
- If they have a concert or program, go! It may not be a big deal to you, but they've put their heart and soul into it even if they act like it's no big deal.
- Display their art work. They are proud of it. Keep a box for just their art work because when they hit 5th or 6th grade, you won't be getting those drawings/paintings. Those messy drawings really show you how they see life. It's through their eyes, and you'll miss that little knowledge when they're old.
- And remember it's not the fancy clothes or expensive gym shoes they'll remember. It'll be your time and encouraging words that they'll remember.

Me: Pretty sure that entire list could be noted as takeaways, but I'll reiterate a few that stood out to me.

Takeaways:

- Be as involved with your kids as you can be.
- Things that seem small and insignificant to you can mean the world to your kids.
- Celebrate the wins, no matter how small.

Kids—especially teenagers—try to play it cool, but people in general want to be loved, appreciated, and noticed.

Chapter 44:
Episode 104 – Special Guest: Military Mom Part 4 – Closing Thoughts

Introduction:

Dear Reader,

Previously, we received some top-notch advice for kid-wrangling. In this final visit with Military Mom, we get to hear the lessons her kids learned from attending multiple schools and receive some assurances about the aftermath of rough times with them.

~Ann

How did things change from when your oldest started school to when your youngest started school?

Military Mom: It's really like having three separate families: the older three then the middle two and the last two. I did everything different for each group of kids.

Did you take different approaches with your children?

Military Mom: All but one of my kids were truly self-motivated and that was son number two. He had a hearing problem which wasn't caught till he was about two.

This meant he didn't have the normal learning of speech till he was maybe three or four, which also meant that when he was in kindergarten and they were learning the ABC's he never caught on.

Then, when he was in 1st grade and learning to read, they stopped teaching phonics, and he had no clue how to pronounce any of the letters which meant he hated reading. And even though he's now forty, he still doesn't cherish the written word.

He can read but he just doesn't enjoy it.

Our youngest daughter was adopted at age two-and-a-half years old. She wasn't really taught English, just mama, daddy, no, and yes. She also had open heart surgery at sixteen months and then was sent to a foster home in China. That foster mom didn't speak English.

Besides not speaking English, our daughter could not walk at all. She was kept in a wicker basket from sixteen months till the time we got her. She was spot on for her age from the waist up, but she had no muscle mass from the waist down, which meant when we came back home the first thing we did was put her into intense occupational and physical therapy.

She also had to be kept back a year in kindergarten because her speech was so far behind. We called it Kindergarten Part 2.

She also had a 90% hearing loss in both ears, which required ear surgery, and again, she missed so much speech development that she was not a reader.

Now though? I can't keep up with her and her books. She is also carrying a 3.91 GPA.

How did your kids spend summer?

Military Mom: That's easy since we're a military family every summer we went to my parents' farm. Then, my parents would have all the relatives over, or we'd work in the tobacco field or garden, take tractor rides, go fishing, hiking, etc.

Family has always been strong with us, and to this day, the kids still visit us during the summer.

Having summer jobs wasn't that important. We believed their *job* was to go to school and get the best grades that they could. When we weren't visiting family, the boys were knee-deep in Boy Scouts. All four boys made Eagle Scout. This was also important to them and us.

Do you have any other closing thoughts?

Military Mom: Going to school is the most important thing your kids will ever do, and they won't always like going.

They'll complain till you'll want to scream because they'd rather play on their phones or laptop instead of sleeping or doing homework. Let them know that everyone has a job and going to school and getting the best grades that they can *IS* their job.

Your job is to make sure they get the most out of it by supporting them and encouraging them even if you could care less about Trig or Physics or Drama Club.

Let them pick extracurricular activities they can have fun with and learn teamwork.

In my opinion, it's not your job to be their friend. It's your job to be a parent.

Being their friend will come later when they are older and ask for advice.

I've seen too many kids who treat their parents like their best friend and most of these kids run all over the parents with no sense of respect that should be given to the parent.

If you do need to move your freshman-senior into a new school, they will act like you're the devil himself and swear they hate you and will never speak to you again. But trust me, after they find new friends, all will be forgiven.

It'll take time, but they truly won't die or stop talking to you. You'll sometimes wish they'd stop talking to you, but they won't. All but my two youngest girls have gone to numerous schools, and they are better for it.

What lessons do you think your kids learned by attending multiple schools?
Military Mom: It makes them self-reliant, outgoing, ask questions of adults, and question things around them.

My two youngest girls went to a language immersion elementary school and learned Mandarin, and they are (or were) going to an engineering high school.

They've learned to ask questions, to think for themselves, to become self-motivated, to do things my other kids never would have thought of.

Can you give us an example?
Military Mom: Things like how to build a car and explain the process to business owners.

Okay, back to your closing thoughts. Last words?
Military Mom: Last, but not least, listen to your kids. Really listen to them. Let them know that if they try their best at something that's what counts, not the grade.

Not every kid is going to ace math or English. Art might be their thing. Praise them for that, but also stress that math and English might be helpful as well.

Don't belittle their talent, just help them improve it. They don't have to like it, but they will thank you for listening to them when they're older.

Kids don't come with instructions, so if you screw up let them know that you're human also.

Me: Thank you for sharing. I think I'd like to hire you as a motivational speaker for my incoming students.

Takeaways:
- Effort counts more than the grade.
- Parenting is not about being your kids' best friend.
- Listen to your kids.
- Not every kid will be a school whiz. Praise kids for the talents they have, but also, let them know math and other subjects have their merits too.
- Nobody's perfect. Apologize when necessary. Forgive when necessary.

Chapter 45:
Episode 105 – Special Guest: MandyReads (Talking about School Transitions)

Introduction:

Dear Reader,

The end of the school year is both exciting and busy.

Please welcome another brave, experienced parent stepping forward to tell us about the many school transitions her kids have gone through.

~Ann

Please give us a little background on your family situation.

MandyReads: We are a family of six. Four girls (ages 21, 19, 15, and 7).

Me: That's a lot of girls.

MandyReads: For the past eight years our girls attended a very small school in Arkansas. Starting in the fall of 2019, our oldest graduated high school and started at SAGU (Southwestern Assemblies of God University. It is a private Christian college in Texas.)

In the fall of 2021, our second oldest followed her sister to SAGU. We decided we wanted to be closer to them, so we moved to Texas as well. There, our fifteen-year-old (14 at the time) was leaving 8th grade, which is junior high in Arkansas, and would be attending middle school in Texas.

High school starts in 9th grade in Texas. We decided to home school her the rest of the year through an online school a friend of ours uses. She would then start high school the following school year. Our seven-year-old. (6 at the time) had started kindergarten in Arkansas but transferred to her new school once we moved.

What was the last milestone your children passed?
MandyReads: We have two high school graduates that have since started college. Our oldest will be starting her fourth year and our second oldest, her second year. Our fifteen-year-old is currently finishing up 8th grade and our seven-year-old has graduated kindergarten.

Why did you choose the schools your kids attended?
MandyReads: Our oldest had toured SAGU starting in 10th grade and was accepted spring of that year. She has a calling to do missions and her minor is in missions.

Our second oldest actually wanted to attend a different AG school in southern Missouri. But once she toured SAGU as well, she changed her mind. Her calling is to be a youth minister, and she would like to do something along the lines of a social worker to help kids in need.

As for the elementary school, it is in our district. But we have enjoyed our new school and the staff so far. Plus side, it is within walking distance.

We chose the online program for our 8th grader based off the recommendation of a friend. It was very short notice, so it was fine for us in a pinch. If I would have had more time, I would have just schooled her myself as the online program is very dated.

Which was the hardest transition for you?
MandyReads: I think the hardest for me as a parent was when our oldest graduated high school and went to college. She has always been a homebody and now she was going to be living five-plus hours away.

Every time we would drop her off or visit and it was time to go, was very hard on all of us. We are such a close family and it hurt leaving each time. Now that we live just an hour away, it's not so bad.

We run down and pick them up or visit for the day. We already knew we were moving to Texas when we were taking our second oldest to SAGU for the first time, so the transition wasn't hard at all.

The next hardest would be sending our youngest to kindergarten. She should have started when she was five in the fall of 2020. But I was hesitant of her going with covid.

I didn't think she would wear a mandatory mask. I decided to wait a year and start her when she was six. But, of course, masks were once again mandatory in Arkansas at the start of the 2021/2022 school year. But she did great and transitioned to Texas just as well.

Which was the easiest transition for you?
MandyReads: I think for me, it was always easiest sending them to kindergarten, besides with our youngest, as I mentioned earlier. They may have been a bit hesitant but excited, too. And once they were there, they had a great time.

I was always so excited for them to start. I knew they would love it.

Did your children do the typical high school rites of passage?

MandyReads: My girls are complete homebodies. They never cared for going to games all that much. One played basketball until 10th grade and then focused on her grades. Another was in choir until she graduated.

They attended homecomings and proms (my second oldest had her prom canceled her junior year because of covid.)

How involved with your kids' schooling are/were you?

MandyReads: Thankfully my girls have all been in Gifted and Talented classes from an early age. I never once had to help them on any of their homework. And most nights they never had it because they got it done in school.

Did your children receive any special services?

MandyReads: So far, three of the four girls have all been in Gifted and Talented classes. Our youngest was tested, but because of her being in kindergarten and switching schools, she didn't get in just yet. But they plan to retest her next year.

They get their smarts honestly from their daddy.

What do you think was the most valuable experience of high school?

MandyReads: For my two oldest, it was a teacher they had and loved.

She was an English/Lit teacher, and she really pushed them to think. While I wasn't a fan of her, they adored her, and I can appreciate that in a teacher. She really had them thinking with each class.

What was the college application process like?

MandyReads: The application to SAGU wasn't hard. And they were accepted pretty quickly.

But the FAFSA was the worst.

Me: FAFSA = Free Application for Federal Student Aid (It's how you get federal loans for college.)

MandyReads: It went fine the first year. But it seemed like the second time we had to fill it out, it was a nightmare.

Then this past year, the school said we messed up on something, and FAFSA said it wasn't so. I don't know what I changed but it ended up fixing the problem. I just dread doing it all over again this year.

Did you visit colleges?

MandyReads: With our oldest we just visited SAGU. With our second oldest we visited SAGU and Evangel.

If you could do it over again, would you change anything?

MandyReads: I honestly think we have done well with each transition and with each girl. So, I don't think I would change anything just yet.

What advice do you have for parents in your situation?

MandyReads: My only advice is to prepare yourself for the FAFSA application ... because it's a mother!!

Takeaways:

- Family is important.
- Filling out the FAFSA sucks.

Chapter 46:
Episode 106 – Special Guest: Almost Done Parent

Introduction:

Dear Reader,

Just as every kid is different. Every parent has their own unique life journey. Kids don't come with an instruction manual.

There's a lesson in everything, so it's always wise to ask questions of those who have traveled a certain path before us.

I'm going to stop there before I get too pithy on you.

Let's hear from our guest.

~Ann

Hi. What would you like me to call you?

Almost Done Parent

Perfect. Can you give us a little background on your family situation?

Almost Done Parent: I'm the mother of three. 24 – Girl, 21 – Boy, 15 – Boy. They all went to public school from kindergarten to high school.

What is your current schooling situation?

Almost Done Parent: My last child will be a Sophomore in the fall.

Why did you choose the schools your kids attended?

Almost Done Parent: I chose the public school because they had a magnet program. Then our schools were unaccredited for a few years, and we couldn't leave the system because they were trying to keep all the kids.

My husband and I couldn't afford private schools, so we chose to make the best out of what we had.

Me: I've never heard of a public school being unaccredited before.

Accreditation bunny trail:

heads to Google

Ah. That explains it. Unaccredited in this context is a reflection of the school district. I'm guessing that means the school is struggling.

Enrollment is a bigger issue in private schools because that's often how they determine what staff they can afford.

Private Christian schools have their own accreditation system. That's what I was confusing this with. Because with all the words in the English language, of course, we're going to use the same one in different context.

Back on track. Which was the hardest transition for you?

Almost Done Parent: The only child I had the hardest transitions with was my youngest. He enjoyed school, he just never wanted to go to school in the morning, so getting him there daily was our biggest issue.

Which was the easiest transition for you?

Almost Done Parent: The other two didn't have any problems with switching schools. They looked forward to it.

Did your children do the typical high school rites of passage?

Almost Done Parent: My daughter played tennis and ran track. She went to all the dances and attended two proms her senior year. My son played basketball. He went to his prom but didn't attend any of the dances. He played an instrument in a choir. He went to a ROTC (Reserve Officer Training Corps) program, so he rose in rank while in high school.

The youngest was in a drama class and is in the ROTC program in high school.

Me: My school never had an ROTC program, but that sounds like fun.

How involved with your kids' schooling are/were you?

Almost Done Parent: I worked fulltime, so most of my activities were after school.

I was the President of the PTO (Parent-Teacher Organization) for ten years. I was on the board of the charter school my youngest attended.

I haven't participated in anything this year for my youngest only because of covid changes.

Did your children receive any special services?
Almost Done Parent: No

What was the college application process like?
Almost Done Parent: Hard because I didn't have a clue, and we waited too late to apply for a lot of colleges for my daughter.

My son decided he didn't want to go to school.

Did you visit colleges?
Almost Done Parent: Yes, we visited two colleges.

If you could do it over again, would you change anything?
Almost Done Parent: I would have started the college process earlier and asked more questions.

I would have sat with my children and discussed college and let them know it was my dream, but it didn't have to be their dream. I know now what to do for my last son. If he doesn't want to go to college, I won't push it.

What advice do you have for parents in your situation?
Almost Done Parent: Listen to your children. Their opinions matter and you will save a lot of money if you listen to them. They will tell you what they want. Don't force them because that's how your family did it or that's what you want. It's their life, not yours.

Do you have any other closing thoughts?
Almost Done Parent: Time goes fast, remember to enjoy the moments because you don't get a second chance.

Me: Definitely true. I'm coming to the end of another year of teaching here. Every year seems to go a little bit faster.

Takeaways:

- Listen to your children.
- Start the college application process early if that's the road your kid wants to take.
- Time goes very fast.
- Cherish every moment.

Chapter 47:
Episode 107 – Special Guest:
Interview with Culinary Teacher

Introduction:

Dear Reader,

Depending on the school, you'll get a wide range of electives.

I'd personally never heard of hospitality classes outside the major in college.

As previously noted, I learned to sew on buttons while I was in high school since there wasn't really a cooking class.

These days, some of my students come straight from culinary. While it's a very cool class, it's kind of a nuisance to have the kids bring food into my lab.

Still, cooking is a vital life skill, and I'm glad students get the chance to learn their way around kitchen appliances. (Knowing some of the kids who have taken that course, that honestly would scare the heck out of me.)

~Ann

What would you like me to call you?
Not sure.

Me: Okay. Guess I'll just go with Culinary Teacher since that seems to be your primary course load.

How many years have you taught?
Culinary Teacher: This will be my 8th year.

Did you have a different career?
Culinary Teacher: Yes. I was a project coordinator for the government for 10 years. I hated it.

Did you have friends in high school?
Culinary Teacher: Yes, some of which I'm still friends with.

Did you get close to any teachers when you were a student?
Culinary Teacher: No.

Why did you choose teaching?
Culinary Teacher:
- Because I love what I teach.
- I love being home with my kids during the summer.
- When my kids aren't in school neither am I.

Me: Those are all excellent reasons.

What classes do you teach?
Culinary Teacher: I teach Hospitality and an Introduction to Culinary to middle school and Culinary 1-4 to high school students.

I also offer a ServSafe Certification Prep that helps students to prepare and pass the ServSafe Certification Test.

Me: *Once again heads to Google to do some research.*

Apparently ServSafe is a Manager Certification test that consists of 40 multiple choice questions. It's there to say that the person had adequate knowledge about foodborne diseases. I'm guessing people need it to work in certain capacities in a restaurant.

How long did it take you to prepare for class?
Culinary Teacher: My first few years took longer to plan but now I have a flow, so it doesn't take as long.

Me: Most forms of teaching have time that isn't always considered on-the-clock. I've seen the culinary teacher at my school hauling shopping bags around. I like grocery shopping, but I think it'd be less fun if I had to buy in bulk for a class.

How do you approach prep?
Culinary Teacher: Networking with other teachers in my subject area.

I also work with other teachers in different subject areas when it comes to helping a student who may need additional help.

They may have a teaching method that works that you haven't thought of.

What kind of school did you work in?
Culinary Teacher: I currently work in a dropout prevention school. We take students who are at risk for dropping out and help them get caught up and graduate.

What was the most preps you had in a year?
Culinary Teacher: 7

Me: Yikes. Being an electives teacher is not for the faint of heart.

What is your favorite class to teach?
Culinary Teacher: Hospitality

What was your favorite topic to teach?

Culinary Teacher: I like all the topics I teach.

What was your least favorite class to teach?

Culinary Teacher: I don't really have a least favorite.

What is the best, worst, and most fun part of teaching?

Culinary Teacher: I love the teaching part of teaching.
Everything else that goes along with it makes it difficult.

- The politics
- The mountains of paperwork
- The pointless trainings
- The constant interruptions
- The endless testing
- The lack of support

Do you have any advice for new teachers?

Culinary Teacher:

- Do not take it personally.
- Pick your battles.
- Network not only with teachers at your school but also other schools. They will be your best resource.

What do you think kids need to succeed at school?

Culinary Teacher:

- Parent involvement
- Teacher involvement

Were you involved in any extracurriculars as a teacher?

Culinary Teacher: Yes, I ran a club called FCCLA.

Me: *Runs to Google yet again.*

FCCLA = Family, Career, and Community Leaders of America

When do you think the emphasis on grades kicks in?
Culinary Teacher: High School when a student wants to go to college.

How did the pandemic affect teaching?
Culinary Teacher: It put a lot of students behind and a school like mine is helping them catch up.

Takeaways:
- Paperwork, politics, and pointless trainings are some of the low points of teaching.
- Interruptions, endless testing, and lack of support are some other low points of teaching.
- Though it's hard, try not to take stuff personally.
- Electives teachers have many preps (different courses to teach).
- There are dropout prevention schools to help students at risk of giving up on school.
- Parent and teacher involvement with students are both key to success.

Chapter 48:
Episode 108 – General Opinion: Dear Cheaters Part 1 – An Open Letter

Introduction:

Dear Readers,

Writing is good for the soul. It's also very cathartic.

There are a lot of things that usually can't—or shouldn't—be said to students in the heat of the moment when you catch them cheating.

We can chat more about the lack of consequences in more detail later, but it's a fact of life in most public schools that consequences are harder and harder to come by.

That leads to three camps: see what you can get away with, do what you're supposed to do because it's the right thing to do, and whatever happens (implied, I don't care).

This letter is meant for the kids in the first camp.

~Ann

Dear Cheater (or kid sorely tempted to cheat on something),

For the record, I'm referring to cheating in the sense of having someone else do your work for you, having extra notes for a test, giving a friend all your answers, and so forth.

While this doesn't directly relate to the relationship you have with your significant other, I would like to point out that your brain is very good at rationalizing. If your brain can greenlight one kind of cheating, it's not a huge leap to think it can and will okay relationship cheating as well.

It's not worth it.

First point: Most forms of cheating are a lot of work.
If you devoted the time, energy, and effort that goes into cheating to the actual assignment, you'd likely have time and energy to spare afterwards.

Second point: Cheating gives a false impression of your progress.
Let's brush all the nonsense that can go with schools away for the moment and focus on the heart of education.

While you may learn a few random facts here and there, school teaches you much more than facts.

Brief look at some other positive lessons you can learn along the way:
- Time management
- How to deal with hard things
- How you personally absorb information

Side note: Chapter 54 has a more complete list of life lessons learned in school.

When you cheat, you often learn lessons, but they may hurt you in the long run.

Here's a short list of things that can (and will likely) happen if you get away with it.

- You get away with it and don't feel a lick of guilt or remorse.
- You get away with it but feel guilty.
- You do it again. (If you get away with it again, you're likely to continue the cycle. It'll become easier to rationalize, and if you're like most people, you'll take greater and greater risks until something bites you in the backside.)

Here's a short list of the things that can happen if you get caught.

- You get caught and yelled at (or get the look of deep disapproval and/or disappointment).
- You get caught, yelled at, and get a 0 for the assignment.
- You get caught, yelled at, get a 0 for the assignment, and get a detention.
- You get caught, yelled at, get a 0, and fail the course.
- You've successfully damaged your reputation.
- You could have other consequences like missing out on the National Honor Society, teacher recommendations, and so forth.

Fortunately for you, people tend to have short memories, and there's a lot going on.

Teachers as a whole are a forgiving lot and used to the things kids try to get away with.

On the other hand, you might be the straw that broke the camel's back. In other words, the teacher might decide to try to get as many consequences to stick to you because the last 200 cheaters got away with it.

You might think that's unfair, and it is. Unfair goes both ways though. Ironically, you getting consequences would be the only thing under the fair side of the comparison chart.

When I asked my students who they're trying to please, some said themselves and some said parents.

Formal assessments (tests) aren't punishment, they're progress markers. One elementary teacher called tests Effort Snitches (Chapter 77). No matter what they're called, that is accurate either way you look at it.

As I said, cheating takes effort.

I usually point out that you wouldn't want to go to a doctor who cheated their way through medical school. (The practical side of me admits that a frightening number of us likely do exactly this.) We—and the cheaters—like to think that everybody learns what they need to when they get to the stuff that counts.

Everything counts. Degree may vary, but everything that happens to you will shape you somehow.

Habits follow you:
Form the type of habits that will help you have the drive and ambition to get where you want to be later in life.

Take pride in the work you do. Although there's a certain amount of skill involved in cheating, it's better to see if you've taken in what was being taught.

A failing grade is a reflection of lack of mastery on a specific something, not a commentary on your worth as a person.
I think people confuse those two points.

Schools combine a lot of things. Sure, some people are great at the school game. They get high grades, play sports, and sing in the choir.

What you're *good at* can be influenced by your interest level, your physical circumstances, and things out of your control.

Do your best. Then, don't worry. If you're not meeting the prerequisites for becoming a brain surgeon, find an equally cool career with different requirements.

Cheating puts teachers in an awkward position:

There are always exceptions, but generally, when you're caught cheating, you place the teacher in the uncomfortable position of deciding what to do. It can be handled inside the classroom or kicked to administration and parents.

A lot of time gets put into weighing what's fair to the cheater and the rest of the class. I'll expand on this in the next chapter.

Closing thoughts:

No one person can do every job ever invented. We need each other. Find something you're passionate about and pour your heart and soul into it.

There's a very big difference between doesn't understand and doesn't try. Teachers can work with the first one, but the second one is much harder to deal with.

It's pithy but true that the most successful people are those who tried and failed at something multiple times. They persevered and found a way, but not on the first shot.

Takeaways:
- Cheating takes effort
- Habits—both good and bad—follow you into your future
- Don't cheat yourself out of accurate representations of what you know
- Don't be afraid to try something and fail at it.
- Cheating puts others in an uncomfortable position.

Chapter 49:
Episode 109 – General Opinion:
Dear Cheaters Part 2 – Some Small
Examples

Introduction:

Dear Reader (and Potential Student Cheaters),

I want to tell you about some of the cheaters I've caught recently. For context, this was the last formal assessment (quiz) of the year. This year, I've let the students have a cheat sheet of information. I teach science, so we have a lot of formulas. I have always given students the main formulas, but I don't always give the other versions of the formulas.

The cheat sheet essentially lets them do some of the algebraic manipulations ahead of taking the test or quiz.

The final exam cheat sheet could have anything they wanted on it, but every other sheet to that point had very specific dos and don'ts.

~Ann

Overview:

Two students in separate classes had the answers to some additional homework problems worked out on either the back or a completely separate sheet.

How they got caught.

Acting shady.

I wasn't even on the lookout for cheating because I knew everybody would have an additional sheet on their desk.

The one kid had two sheets, so as I randomly walked around the room, he moved a book on top of the second sheet (the one he shouldn't have had.)

The other kid had stuff written on both sides of the sheet. So, I caught the movement of flipping things over to check the back side.

What happened after they got caught?

During the quizzes, I didn't make a big deal of it.

I just took the sheets with too much information away and told them they'd get a 0 for that quiz. It happened that for that set, I was giving a quiz on two topics and accepting the higher of the two scores anyway, so they still had a chance to earn points.

How did the students respond?

One kid said nothing.

The other kid spent some time writing a sincere apology on the back of his quiz. He also asked for the chance to do a makeup.

For the record, that is a decent way of handling it.

After grading both students' quizzes, it turns out that the one who said nothing already scored higher on the other quiz, so a retake was a moot point. The one who apologized had a 75 on the side with the additional notes—the one I zeroed—and a 40 on the other side.

I weighed the options and decided to let the 0s stand.

Out of curiosity, I asked my colleagues for their opinions.

Here are the results:

- One colleague said they might zero the quiz depending on how much they liked the kid because at this point (late in the year) you can play favorites if you want to. The apology note would factor into that calculation.
- The same colleague said my options were to let it slide ("it's the end of the year and I don't have the energy") or hit them with the zero ("let it be a learning lesson of don't suck.")
- Another colleague asked what zeroing the grade would do. I did the calculation. At the time, it would set the kid for an 82.4 (which is a B⁻). After hearing that, this colleague said to leave the 40 in place (the score the kid earned on the other quiz).
- This colleague said to leave it even if I liked the kid and he apologized because sometimes sorry isn't good enough.

How the story ended:

I left the 0 for the first quiz, giving the kid the 40 he earned on the other quiz. His marking period score was just shy of that B until I put in some participation scores. Once those were in, it bumped up to an 83.

I did not let him do a retake because that would be more work for me. There's no reason I should be doing more work because he messed up in terms of judgment. I'd already lost time having to weigh out consequences, surveying friends, and composing an answer.

I believe if I'd entered the score he'd "earned" on the quiz he cheated on, the student would have ended up with an 87 for the marking period.

In the grand scheme of things, going from a B^+ prospect to a B is going to make zero difference. He's still an overall good student.

Did the apology matter?
It was a nice touch and certainly didn't hurt.

Technically, I would have been within my rights to zero the grade completely (as in not even distinguish the two grades) on principle of there being a cheating incident.

I think the compromise of letting that other score stand worked out well for all parties.

Dear Cheaters (and those tempted to cheat),
I know it can seem like you don't have much choice because you must earn a certain grade for whatever reason.

Just think twice before you do anything.

Dealing with cheaters is not a fun position for any teacher to be in. (Oh, I'm sure there's always the odd exception of somebody who relishes the power, but that's not the norm.) Most people just want to teach a subject they love and wait for that spark to light up a kid's eyes.

Some people feel bad about having to zero out a score or tell parents and administrators. In a way, it's just painful to watch people make avoidable mistakes. It can come down to a weighty decision to save a kid from themselves here and now or hope they'll learn from consequences.

Don't give someone that kind of power over you. It is your choice to cheat, but once you get caught at it, you force someone to make hard decisions.

There are greater consequences that people don't want to hand out to you. When you get to college, stuff like that can lose you scholarships and get you kicked off teams or removed from programs.

Takeaways:

- I chose to go with a compromise when faced with two students caught cheating.
- I'm hoping the apology was sincere, and the student won't cheat on future things. He's no longer in my class, and every teacher handles these things differently.
- Being the disciplinarian is never a fun job (to the vast majority of teachers).
- I really hope students think ahead and consider the consequences of being caught cheating. The potential ramifications get greater as one gets older.

Chapter 50:
Episode 110 – General Opinion: On Contacting Teachers in the Summer (Spoiler Version Just Don't)

Introduction:

Dear Reader,

Almost titled this one Dear Crazy Parent.

The end of a school year is a bittersweet time. It heralds a transition to summer schedules, wrapping up grades, and moving on.

It's inevitable that the majority of kids want to do well. Likewise, parents (and teachers) want to see the students succeed.

However, asking to discuss grades after the close of a school year puts the teacher in a very awkward position. (Some won't even answer you over the summer, but many of us do check email obsessively even during the summer.)

This chapter will focus specifically on contact after the year has closed, but I should also do a chapter on teachers having personal boundaries.

(I've heard of stories of parents following teachers to their cars to discuss a child's end-of-the-year grade.)

~Ann

Is there an acceptable post-year email?
Sure. If you're up for it and genuinely feel it, a simple thank-you-and-have-a-nice-summer sort of contact is perfectly acceptable.

What kind of email should be avoided?
- Overall grade discussions
- What went wrong on the final discussions – You may genuinely wish to know, but your child is likely the only one you need to question about this.
- Other kids' performances discussions

Sample letter based on ones actually received. (No names. No specifics. Gender picked at random.)
Dear (insert teacher's name),

I wanted to talk with you about my child's final grade. He did so well all year.

We were disappointed that he failed the final exam and ended the year with an overall B-. (He earned a B or higher on all other finals.)

I know he studied for the exam.

He told me it was a difficult final and that many other students struggled on this test.

Can you give me some context on how the kids did in general and what you think went wrong for my son? You can also call me at (insert phone number).

Have a nice summer. Thanks.

Sincerely, me (insert parent name)

My response and a few points:
End of the year grades should be final.
After the grades are submitted, there's not much up for discussion. This sample letter didn't specifically ask for a grade change, but I personally have had people ask for such in the past.

I know of at least one colleague who got asked to change the grade this year based on a request from special services. We can talk about that mess someday if you like.

I'm only mentioning that because to people not in education, it can seem like a foreign concept for people to ask for grade changes because that sort of defeats the purpose of earning a score.

Teachers cannot comment about other kids' performances.
I know there is comfort in knowing other people are in the same position as your child, but legitimately, the performance of other students is no business but their own and maybe their parents.

Subjects can't be fairly compared.
Arts and sciences are generally assessed differently.

Gifts side note: While there are people who can seemingly do everything, traditional school heavily favors those who learn best by audio and visual styles. Besides some electives, school also misses a wide range of skills.

My point is people should always do their best, but if that still translates to a C (average score), it doesn't matter.

Some people excel at putting essays together in short notice. That skill won't help you much on a multiple choice formal assessment. The reverse is also true. Some people excel at traditional assessments but struggle to piece words together quickly enough in a timed essay.

Even between two sciences, you can't compare performance. There are too many variables.

Test performance can be affected by:

Please note, these are suggestions only. It's doubtful every factor came into play.

- Preparation time – This can be affected by where in the schedule a particular final is and what else the student has to take that day. Even with a break, if it's the second exam, the student may not do as well as they would like.
- Student health and alertness while taking the test. Let's face it, if you're not feeling well, your test scores can suffer.
- Room conditions (Might not seem like a big factor, but some schools aren't air conditioned. If the room is uncomfortably hot, one may not be thinking as clearly as they would under peak conditions.)
- Student didn't prepare as well as he or she should have.
- Student expected to fail, so didn't try their best.
- There wasn't adequate time to prepare for the final.
- The kid has intense test anxiety.
- The teacher forgot to tell the students about a large section that would be covered.

What went wrong in this case?

The student ...

- Got a lot of the multiple choice wrong.
- Left a lot of questions blank.

That kind of discussion could be fine, but in email form, it's hard to read context. Teachers are automatically put on the defensive.

Side note (because I don't think it's discussed enough):

There are teachers with anxiety. They are stellar at covering for it, but I mention it because parent contact over grades usually isn't a fun thing for any teacher. That's doubly true for those with certain kinds of anxiety because every word has to be weighed, measured, re-evaluated, re-framed, and double-checked.

Random points:
Kids lie (or stretch the truth).

To be fair, nobody wants to look bad.

There is a big temptation to give you an answer you want to hear. (If my mother asked me if I tried my best, I'd have to be super hard-pressed to answer, "Nah, just winged it.")

But everybody else failed may or may not be true, and in the end, it doesn't matter. Your child is responsible for their grade.

Some kids don't learn to play the partial credit game well. Teachers cannot award points if the question is blank. Even if there is a wrong but ultimately logical answer, something can be given for the effort.

A B⁻ is a respectable grade.

Responsibility matters more than letter grades.

Colleges care about grades, but that's only one factor for consideration. Besides, college isn't the only way to have a successful future. Trades are highly underrated.

Takeaways:
- Parent contact over grades is usually not a lot of fun. It goes with the territory. However, once the year closes, let it end with grace. If it didn't go the way you'd like it to go, resolve to do better next chance and move on.
- Students are responsible for their own grades.

- Comparisons shouldn't be made to other classes or to other students.
- One of the biggest life lessons students should be getting out of their educations is responsibility. That is undermined if you simply ask for a grade handout.

Chapter 51:
Episode 111 – General Opinion:
Asking and Answering Questions

Introduction:

Dear Reader,

Sometimes it may seem like anybody brave enough to answer questions is a mythical creature, but they exist.

Sometimes, they're a tad shy and require more wait time. (That just means you give the students some extra processing time to gain confidence to answer.) But mostly, it's an either or thing.

Every class has a reliable question answerer. They're awesome.

Some of the most challenging students this year answered questions for me.

I was going to focus the chapter around reliable question answerers, but it became more of a tutorial on how to overcome a fear of speaking up in class.

~Ann

Questions are still an integral part of education.
Even if the lesson is structured to minimize the amount of lecture-based direct instruction, asking and answering questions is the best way to learn.

These days, the internet makes it incredibly easy to find information, be it trivial or serious. You do have to weed through some nonsense to get to real information. You also need to be aware of the biases of whoever is presenting the information. Still, the point remains that there is a lot of information available.

Who is the reliable question answerer?
Generally, they're the better students. By that I mean, the ones who score B and above, but that's not an absolute rule. In fact, I'd say three of my question answerers this past year were solid C students.

Philosophical grade aside:
Although I personally wouldn't want a C, it's not the end of the world.

As long as students put in genuine effort, I've designed my course such that the vast majority of students should have zero problems passing.

If someone earns a C, that's fine. It can mean anything from that's the peak of their ability in the course to having a lot of other stuff going on in their lives to the student is just floating along.

What kind of personality does the reliable question answerer have?
The three that spring into mind first are outgoing, but I did also have at least one very quiet student who also ventured answers. If she wasn't answering a question, I don't think I heard her voice the entire school year. (She didn't even answer me during attendance.)

So, what's the common factor?

I think most students who offer answers to questions have confidence. This can be confidence in their academic skills or a general devil-may-care projected attitude about what others think.

Why do teachers love having a reliable question answerer?

It can be very difficult to pose a question and have twenty students stare back at you. (Okay, so three stare back and the others are on their phones. Same difference. You're being ignored.)

Offering answers vs. answering when called upon:

Many students know the correct answers yet never offer them. Offering would be the student raises their hand, indicating that they wish to share the answer. Answering when called upon is still great, but try not to wait.

Delicate balance:

Teachers are supposed to include every student in the lesson as much as possible. This includes questioning strategies that engage students.

You have to balance this with the idea that there are times you won't get anything done if nobody answers. Therein lies the temptation to always call on the reliable kid. Even if they're wrong, you have the chance to turn it into a learning moment.

It's okay to get answers wrong:

Nobody expects students to be immediate experts in every lesson they're taught. The expectation is you do your best.

Education's often about the hidden lessons and that invaluable life lesson of learning how to learn.

What is learning?

I'm sure I can Google a formal definition, but essentially, it's absorbing information in such a way that you can use it.

Problem solving doesn't necessarily mean math problems.

We problem solve all the time.

If you press on a door and it doesn't budge, you instinctively press harder. When that doesn't work, you may try checking a lock or pulling. It's a simple example, but that's problem solving.

Reasons to not like answering questions:

- Fear of getting something wrong
- Fear of looking foolish or stupid
- Fear of drawing attention to oneself
- Fear of what others will think
- Didn't pay attention, so genuinely doesn't know the answer
- Thinks the lesson is dumb and won't ever be used later in life

Observation:

That's a whole lot of fear.

Are there bad questions?

Sometimes.

Samples:

- Off-topic – Some teachers are more laid back. Some are also the cause of off-topic discussions. (What's your favorite food? What are you doing this weekend?)

Note: Timing is everything. Expressing an interest in someone and indulging in pleasantries are worthwhile pursuits, but you're better off keeping that to the beginning or end of class.

- May I use the restroom, get a drink, take a walk, etc.? – Can't tell you how many times, I think maybe this is the day that one kid is going to offer an answer to a question and get completely disappointed.

Note: Sometimes, I make the student answer the question anyway before they leave the room. (Again, there's nothing inherently wrong with a question, but I question their sense of timing.)

How to become a better question answerer:
- If you're afraid of getting the question wrong, wait for the low-hanging fruit.

Note: Teachers will often scale questions. When an initial question is too difficult, the teacher will ask a few other questions that are easier.

In my class, there are quite a few answers that only require a little bit of calculator work once the problem is established to a certain point.
- Ask your own questions. Engaging is still participating. Odds are good others also have that question.
- Ask and answer questions as often as you can. It gets easier as you form the habit.
- Train yourself to do it if you must. By that, I mean purposefully try to answer one question, then two, then three.
- You may not always be called upon.
- If you have a specific problem with answering questions aloud, come up with an alternative. (For example, answer all the questions you can in your notes or on a separate piece of paper. With some exceptions, your education rests in your hands.)
- Put the fears into perspective.

Random points about fears:
- People are usually too self-absorbed to care whether or not you can answer a question.
- People have the same fears as you do.

- Things you know are much less scary. Same holds true for answering questions.

Takeaways:
- The more you ask questions, the easier it will become.
- There are always easy questions spread throughout a class. Jump on those if you want to ease yourself into answering questions.

Chapter 52:
Episode 112 – Special Guest: Dr. Mom Talks about Virtual School Part 1

Introduction:

Dear Reader,

Someone once told me that children are your most prized possession.

This is true. You want what's best for them.

It can be incredibly frustrating to have to deal with overcrowded school systems because then there is a tendency for things to fall by the wayside. That means you—the parent—need to step up your advocating game or find an alternative.

Our present guest did exactly that—she found a free public virtual school that allowed her kids to flourish.

~Ann

Quick definition clarification:
I'm going to be using the term virtual school here instead of home school even if it takes place mostly at home.

Home school – Requires registering as a home school situation in most cases. May involve a cohort. Works with home school curriculum.

Virtual school – Still run by the state. There are outside teachers involved in creating the curriculum, handing out assignments, grading things, and so forth.

The difference between that and a normal public school is that virtual school requires little to no in-person presence. For certain students, this is a wonderful change.

What would you like me to call you?
Dr. Mom.

Me: That works great.

What was your schooling background?
Dr. Mom: I went to a brick-and-mortar K-12. I was an honors and AP student and thrived well in high-level learning.

What kind of virtual school do your kids attend?
Dr. Mom: They attend a free, online public school.

Why did you decide to send your kids to virtual school?
Dr. Mom: We made the choice during COVID to move both teenagers to online learning.

Our district didn't really take COVID or any protocols seriously. As a parent, it is my responsibility to make sure that my kids are protected, educated, and confident in their education.

There's also the fact that I am immunocompromised, and my kids were both afraid that attending in person would put me at risk.

However, once we moved online, we realized that it was a great success for both children and gave them more of a life outside the classroom.

They had the opportunity to go back in person and did for one week.

During that week, the in-person experience was horrid.

Bullying at the local high school is extreme and not really addressed by administration.

They weren't receiving the best high school experience that led to anxiety, stress, and unnecessary panic attacks.

So, we moved them to Connections Academy and haven't looked back.

Me: I'm glad you found the right fit for them.

Do you have a career in addition to helping your kids with virtual school?
Dr. Mom: Yes. I am self-employed and manage multiple different businesses.

How involved with your kids' schooling are you? Do you have a routine?
Dr. Mom: I am very involved.

Their school requires that I give attendance daily and approve any work they submit.

The kids and I meet at the beginning of each week to determine a plan of action, identify what is a priority, follow up on missing work, and set a routine for the week.

Every night at dinner we talk about their day, offer assistance if needed and expand the conversation beyond the textbook information.

If I have concerns or questions, I am able to reach out to the teachers, admin, or other school personnel directly.

How does their virtual schoolwork?
Dr. Mom:
- Each teen has access to a dashboard and calendar.
- Each class lists the assignments for the week, any live lessons available, teacher office hours and due dates.
- They log in, go to live lectures or watch the recording for that class if there was overlap or they couldn't make the live session.
- They look at what is due for each class, read the text, do assignments, write papers, reach out to teachers as needed, and submit work/tests all online.
- There is some flexibility on due dates, and they are allowed to submit late work if needed.
- Each semester, we go to parent/teacher conferences via phone.

Me: I think these kinds of schools got more popular during the pandemic. I can see that working well for most classes.

During the pandemic, we didn't do labs in science courses. There are some virtual labs. It's not quite the same, but a decent substitute.

How do you handle getting your kids around other kids (socialization)?
Dr. Mom: My daughter dances with a local studio, volunteers, and does girl scouts.

My son has a group of friends he hangs out with after school and on weekends that all live within a mile of each other.

We encourage them to go out and be teenagers.

Me: Formal, in-person schools do have a lot of wasted time. Besides assemblies, you have attendance taking, crowd control moments, teenage drama, and such.

Out of a forty-five-minute class period, you might only get thirty-five productive minutes.

It's a known fact that the smaller the class size, the more effective teaching can be. When you move to a virtual setting, you're essentially making it a class size of 1.

If you have the proper support from home, this can be a fantastic arrangement.

Videos and virtual conferences are such a prevalent part of life that turning both into learning tools has become the norm. It's therefore not that much of a stretch to have it be the primary way of communicating with teachers.

Takeaways:
- We got two main reasons Dr. Mom chose virtual school: covid and bullying.
- We got a quick rundown on how one virtual school works.
- Though school is the main way many kids socialize, it is not the only way available.

Chapter 53:
Episode 113 – Special Guest: Dr. Mom Talks about Virtual School Part 2

Introduction:
Dear Reader,

We're going to pick right up where we left off with Dr. Mom. She was telling us about why she and her husband chose virtual school for their two kids.

This time, we'll go into more of the reasons behind why virtual school works for her family.

~Ann

How was your experience with the special needs services at your kids' former school? Can you tell us how that has affected your children's education?
Dr. Mom: My daughter is an Aspie. (That means she has Asperger's syndrome.)

She is socially awkward and gets overwhelmed in large crowds or unknown situations.

Moving to virtual school was the best option for her because it gave her full control of her schedule, her routine, when she attends school and when she needs to take breaks.

It allows her to be a teenager with less stress of trying to fit in.

What challenges arose when dealing with the school?
Dr. Mom: The biggest challenge we had at the brick-and-mortar high school was the ridiculously large population of the school.

- There were so many kids that sometimes there weren't enough seats in a classroom for all the students.
- Walking down any hallway during passing period was dangerous.
- Bullying was high and very little, if anything was ever done to stop it by administration or teachers.

Once we moved to the virtual school, life for both teens became great.

Can you tell us about your kids' schooling journeys?
Dr. Mom: Both of my teenagers are in Gifted.

I had to write a formal letter to the district to force them to test them.

For years, it was a constant fight to get the school to see that there was an exceptional need.

Once place in Gifted, while still in middle school, the Gifted teacher was phenomenal at meeting each kid where they were at and pushing them just a little outside their comfort zone, while providing a safe space.

At the high school brick-and-mortar, this was not the case.

Once we moved to virtual school, both kids were receiving what they needed.

My daughter attends social work once a week to help with her awkwardness.

The school works closely with us to make sure that both kids are getting what they need.

Working with the administration, both kids were able to enroll at the community college this summer. The virtual HS allows them to use college credit to earn high school credit.

Both kids will graduate a year early, each as a junior due to the support of the school and the ability to go to college while in high school.

Going to school virtually has helped both excel in the online college courses due to consistency in learning.

What's the hardest part of running virtual school?
Dr. Mom: Honestly, making sure they have all of the classes needed to graduate.

Other than that, making sure they are socializing outside of the classroom and still getting the normal high school experience.

What is the best, worst, and most fun part of teaching?
Dr. Mom:
- I feel the best part of virtual school is being able to go out into the community and take field trips/learning experiences as a family as it relates to the curriculum or what they are learning this semester.
- The only worst part is the lack of connection/socializing in person. However, that is expected to get better now that COVID restrictions have decreased.
- The school plans in-person gatherings each semester.

- The most fun part of teaching is being able to engage with my teens, see what they are passionate about and what inspires them.

Do you have any advice for people considering virtual school as an option?
Dr. Mom:
- The best advice I can give is to do what is best for your kids.
- Forget what society and others say.
- Focus on what they need right now in this moment, and how you can help them achieve the goals they set for themselves.

What are the advantages of virtual school?
Dr. Mom: They had ample free time to do hobbies, go out and explore, travel during school days, sleep in, or (for my son) play video games.

It took the stress out of school and took away the excess time kids often sit in classrooms doing nothing. We basically were able to increase their productivity and decrease wasted time in school. It's been amazing.

Did you get any advice when you were just starting out on the journey? What do you think of that advice (if applicable)?
Dr. Mom: Not really, but I come from years of working in higher education and K-12.

I understood the importance of meeting my kids where they were at, helping them expand their knowledge, and providing it in a format that best fits them, regardless of what is normal or "in."

The age of my teens helped me have open, honest conversations with them to make sure that this was the right fit.

After finishing out Year 2 online, we have no regrets.

I am grateful for the school they attend, the teachers that genuinely care about each of my teens, the counselor that allows me to ask questions, and the administration that strives to provide the best educational experience for everyone.

What advice do you have for parents who are in similar situations or just starting to help their kids navigate the school system?
Dr. Mom:
- If the virtual school has tutorials available, go through them. Explore the website.
- Find out who your "person" is at the school and be willing to ask questions, understanding that the only dumb question is the one not asked.
- Be willing to admit you don't know the answer and take time to find it.
- Use a planner for each kid or print out their weekly schedule with class info and due dates.
- Set up a time each week to talk to your kid(s) individually about their classes.
- Ask them what they liked, didn't like, need more help with, aren't sure of, wish they knew more about and so on.
- Your job as a parent is to support them, engage them in meaningful conversations and help them make lasting connections.
- In the end, you do what is best for your family, regardless of what others you know think or say. They aren't responsible for your kids and their learning. YOU are. Make the most of it.

What do you think kids need to succeed at school?
Dr. Mom: Open communication, parental guidance and support, and a good understanding of why.

- Why we do what we do.
- Why it is important.
- Why we matter.

That list goes on.

Takeaways:

- Virtual school allows for higher productivity with less wasted time. This gives kids more of a chance to be kids.
- Communication is important.
- Regardless of the kind of school, kids need parental support.
- Asking questions is the best way to get answers.

Side note: Virtual school will not work for all kids and all family situations. Dr. Mom was/is uniquely qualified for keeping her kids on track, and this situation fit them well. Not every parent has the same time, energy, and skillset to make it work well. Find the right system for you and your kid(s).

Chapter 54:
Episode 114 – Special Guest: College Photography Prof's Journey Part 1 – History

Introduction:

Dear Reader,

I've said it before, and I'll say it again: everybody has a unique journey.

It's not often that I get somebody to share their life experience in such glorious detail.

Our next guest's love of history and writing and pretty much arts in general, clearly shines through his responses.

I hope you enjoy his tale. He has come far and has a lot to teach us.

~Ann

What would you like me to call you during this interview?

Former student currently working as a college photography teacher and jazz musician.

Me: I'm going to go with College Photography Prof – short for College Photography Professor who is also a jazz musician with a fascinating school history and stellar advice to give.

What was your schooling situation?

College Photography Prof: My K-12 education was public school in the San Francisco East Bay Area.

Graduation date was in 1969.

Additional personal history:

College Photography Prof: High school was not a great educational experience for me because my circle of friends weren't scholastically inclined.

Me: We say peer pressure so often that we don't think much about the power in the people we surround ourselves with.

College Photography Prof: My parents never checked to see if I was doing well in school. As long as I wasn't making trouble, I was on my own.

There were no mentors for me in high school.

If I'd shown more interest in my studies, teachers would have shown more interest in me.

Me: Likely true. As a teacher, I like to think that I'd reach out to the disinterested kid, but it's difficult to know who's just waiting for that spark of interest and who's going to be an energy black hole.

College Photography Prof: I left high school at age 16 and went right into two 2-year colleges at the same time. Being in a new environment with people of all ages that were attending school because they wanted to, not because they had to put me in a new frame of mind.

When I showed the slightest inclination to pursue a subject, my teachers were anxious to mentor me. This change in attitude was partly due to being in an adult environment and mostly due to not getting stoned.

Staying straight brought the world into focus. I started doing well in college right from the start. I enjoyed everything more.

Me: It's easy to think we're invincible, but everything we put into our bodies and minds influences us. This includes drugs, social media input, and negativity in general.

College Photography Prof: I pursued music studies at Chabot College in Hayward, California and Photography at Laney College in Oakland, California and graduated with both degrees at the same time.

This may seem like a big feat, but there were lots of lower division requirements that were recognized by both colleges, so it was really just 1.5x work, not double.

There were a lot of live music clubs back then and my band played out two nights a week. I was a mediocre guitar player and a good photographer.

My photo instructor at Laney College recommended me to some local newspapers, and I began doing simple assignments. I couldn't keep up with photography and music, so I chose photography.

A big reason I chose photography was because I could make more money, and I liked the challenge.

Music didn't make much money, there were many people better

than me, and I didn't like the rejection from being average.

Me: That's excellent logic. Both are difficult to make a living at, so it makes perfect sense that you'd throw your time, energy, and effort into the more lucrative profession.

College Photography Prof: I excelled at photography and became obsessed with getting better and better. I worked very hard at gaining photography skills and it impressed my employers and clients.

Just after my 17th birthday, I landed a job as a photographer with United Press International, the biggest news service in the world in 1971.

I was the youngest person they had ever hired. My first assignment was to cover the *Hippie Invasion of Europe*, which was a terrific adventure.

With no travel experience I suddenly found myself traveling alone through foreign countries having to figure out currencies, communicate with non-English speaking people, find lodging, and get great photos of the changing social scene. There was a lot happening back then, and I was right in the middle of it.

Me: Sounds like a very intriguing challenge. Glad you overcame each challenge and made it back safely to tell the tale.

College Photography Prof: I continued with my photography studies while working as a photojournalist and graduated with two bachelor's degrees from Brooks Institute of Photography.

After getting cholera while photographing an epidemic in Morocco, contacting malaria in northern Thailand, being jailed in Spain, and having a camera shot out of my hands at a political demonstration in the Philippines, I decided to pursue safer avenues of photography.

Me: See now, that's a little too much adventure for me. Have you considered writing a memoir?

College Photography Prof: I opened a photo studio in San Francisco and eventually opened studios in New York and Hong Kong.

These were in the years before digital photography, back when a competent film photographer could make a good living.

Me: Thanks for sharing your personal history with us. Let's shift gears and focus on the nitty-gritty details of your high school experience.

How big was your school?
College Photography Prof: High School was 2000 students.

Very integrated inter-racial student body.

I feel fortunate that my school was in a middle-class area with no absurdly rich kids or desperately poor kids. Either there was no significant race and economic discrimination, or I didn't notice it. My close friends included Black kids, exchange students from Asia, European kids, and Latin American students.

Gangs, snotty kids, and dangerous situations were not an issue. High school was a safe place.

Can you describe a typical day of school?
College Photography Prof: At high school my attendance and timeliness were good.

I walked two miles to and from high school every day until I was a junior and bought a motorcycle.

There were a few good teachers that inspired me, and one or two teachers that really didn't like me, and the feeling was mutual. I did poorly in those classes but didn't fail.

The inspiring teachers found ways to make their subjects interesting, and I responded to them quite well. They had a way of seeing their students as individuals and young adults. Their students wanted to please them.

Me: Contrary to most chapters, I'm going to end with a big fat TO BE CONTINUED because there's a lot more to unpack from this current guest.

Takeaways Part 1:
- Love what you do, but also, pursue the lucrative passions you have.
- Show when you are interested in something, teachers respond well to student interest.

Chapter 55:
Episode 115 – Special Guest: College Photography Prof's Journey Part 2 – Advice

Introduction:

Dear Reader,

Welcome back.

Our current guest, College Photography Professor, just got through sharing an overview of sorts where his educational journey has led. He briefly touched upon what held him back in high school and has some top-notch advice for students about to enter the murky high school waters.

Even though there are many differences between the school world he faced and the current school environments, we can learn from the wisdom he shares.

~Ann

How did you get your socializing in?

College Photography Prof: I had a crowd of guys that I hung out with before class, at lunch, and often after school.

They were musicians and we played music a lot. I participated on the track team, and made friends there, but I was wrongly accused of playing a prank on a coach and was suspended from the team. That turned me off to sports.

The teacher later learned I was not involved in the stunt, but he didn't apologize. And I never rejoined any sports teams. Even after 50 years, I still hold a grudge about that.

Smoking pot often with friends after school and on the weekends was common. Pot made the normally confusing time of adolescence much more difficult than it needed to be.

All kids at that age (13-17) have mood swings, depression, feelings of insecurity, and a strong desire to be accepted. I am quite sure I would have enjoyed my teens much more if I hadn't experienced it through the distorted lens of drugs and drinking.

I was not a dedicated student and performed below my capabilities. As is common for many kids, I thought being a *top student* was not cool.

Smoking pot contributed to my inability to concentrate on schoolwork that I could have enjoyed.

Me: Hindsight is always better than the current moment. We like to think *never me – I won't fall victim to whatever*.

Brief aside: The trappings around school may have changed (tech advances and the like), but kids are still kids. They have many of the same concerns and vulnerabilities young people have had for eons. (Fitting in. Being liked.)

What was the best and worst part of school?
College Photography Prof: The best part of school was interfacing with skilled and dedicated teachers.

Teachers in history, music, photography, and creative writing were the best for me, and I looked forward to their classes. The assignments were fun. Seeing my friends on a daily basis gave me a feeling of belonging that was great.

The worst part of school was attending classes that held no interest for me, where I did poorly. Half of the problem was having mediocre teachers, and the other half was my laziness.

Did you have a favorite subject?
College Photography Prof: All the classes involving creative thinking were enjoyable.

My favorites were:
- Photography
- Art
- Music
- English
- History

What advice do you have for students who might be new to the public school system?
College Photography Prof: I advise students to avoid people that are into counterproductive activities including:
- Making fun of others
- Taking drugs or drinking
- Bullying
- Often angry and blaming others
- Stressful home lives
- Argumentative or angry kids

I recommend associating with kids that are generally happy and well-adjusted. These don't have to be the nerdy top students, but they should be kids that are friendly, honest, and dependable.
- Kids who share your interests.
- Kids that have goals.

- Kids that don't do stuff they know is wrong.

What worked out well for you?

College Photography Prof: Figuring out what really excited me and finding people and companies willing to pay me to do it. That is the most important advice I can give to anyone.

What did you struggle with?

College Photography Prof: Being in a service business for myself was a struggle.

Clients wanted my services, not the services of my employees. This stretched me thin.

Self-owned businesses that involve non-creative services, like specialty retail or car repair, can make money.

But if it's an artistic field you want to pursue, I recommend getting a job with an established company and working there for years until you find a niche that you can pursue on your own.

Me: Hmm. Never thought of it like that. It's an interesting and very true point. I know of people who outsource their author services, and the practice never sat well with me. This clarifies things a smidge.

Additional career advice:

- Research possible careers early in your life.
- Age 14 is a good time to look at various careers. If you think you want to be a doctor, ask a doctor if you can visit them at work and see what it's like. Want to be an astronomer? Call an astronomer and set up a visit.
- Believe me, 90% of the people that get contacted by a kid with questions about career choices are going to make time to see you and speak honestly with you.
- Don't be shy and wait for someone to arrange a field trip. Get out there and ask questions.

- Every time you strike out on your own and learn something important, you'll know things that others do not. That approach will serve you well.

When I was in my early teens, I rode my bicycle around to different businesses and asked questions.

I visited architects, doctors, retailers, real estate offices, gyms, factories, airports, etc.

People will take time to show a kid around. Honest. It's hard to get the courage to do it, but after the first few times, it becomes fun. I recommend it.

Would you have done anything different?
College Photography Prof:
- I would have avoided drugs and drinking. It altered my behavior and held me back.
- I would have chosen to associate with happy people in high school and beyond.
- I would have bought stocks with my extra money. Seems boring, but in the long run, it will provide big returns.

Me: I should just slap a takeaways label over that last section, but I also want to include some points you mentioned previously.

Takeaways:
- Avoid drinking, drugs, and other things that will hinder your educational progress.
- Research careers early in life. Ask questions. People are usually happy to help students get a better understanding of their careers. (Ironically, teaching experiences vary widely, as you can tell if you've read enough of this series.)
- Surround yourself with people who lift you up.
- Invest in your future early.

Chapter 56:
Episode 116 – Social Media Buzz: Evolution of Teacher Talk

Introduction:

Dear Reader,

I spend plenty of time online for promotion purposes, but I don't usually keep up with too much social media dealing with school issues.

I do follow a few accounts because they are usually hilarious.

The following is some of the highlights for a prompt about stuff teachers say that they would not have said 30 years ago.

(And my comments, of course.)

~Ann

Note: The bullet points are either direct quotes or paraphrased. I'm not outing any specific person, and I consider all this information public knowledge since it was posted to a social media platform for anybody to see. If you dig deep enough, you could probably find the prompt and the hundreds of responses.

Second note: Sarcasm runs strongly in many statements. Skip the chapter if that's going to bother you.

Technology:
- Cameras on and mics off.
- Don't make me mute you.
- Get your chrome books out.
- You're supposed to be working on your project, not making TikToks.

Me: I find it painful to admit that high school was twenty-plus years ago. We had computers, but TikTok (2016) was not a thing. Even YouTube (2005) came about during my college years. Zoom (2011) and Facebook (2003) weren't things either.
- Leave your iPads, phones, drugs, and weapons in the box by the door. You can retrieve them at the end of the day.
- Will whoever chose "deez nuts" and "ur mom" for their Kahoot player name please change them. (1 minute later...) Will player "deez" and player "nuts" kindly change their names.

Me: Kahoot names do tend to light the creativity fires in some students.

Food delivery:
- No, you cannot DoorDash a Starbucks order because you got up late and need your coffee.

Me: Although there's a temptation to say, yo, order me something too. The convenience of food delivery is a relatively new concept. (DoorDash – 2013, Uber Eats 2014)

Again, it's not so much the existence of the thing as the attitude of entitlement that accompanies the presumption that anytime—including the middle of class—if I want something, I can get it.

Cell phones:

- Put your phone away.
- Please tell your mother to stop texting you.
- No, you can't call your mom right now. We're in the middle of class.

Me: I've definitely had this conversation with kids. One was having a freakout because he got something on his shorts. He wanted his mom to bring him a new pair.

Cell phones are sort of the bane of high school teachers' existence. It's not so much the item itself as lack of impulse control on the students' part. The all-access attitude that comes with them, and terrible timing.

School violence:

- Teacher, when do we practice hiding from the bad people? (This was said by a first grader.)

Me: I believe that one question carries a whole load of heartbreak. Without opening a messy debate about gun rights, I think everybody can agree that it's just sad for a six-year-old to be concerned about *hiding from bad guys.*

- I know he brought a gun to school and threatened to kill a bunch of you, but it was ONLY an air gun, so he was just suspended for 3 days. I'm sure he didn't really mean he wanted to kill you. He was probably just triggered, and we don't want to hurt his feelings by giving him an actual consequence.

Boundaries:

- Don't call me bro.
- After school is out, a parent asked, "May I add you to Facebook because my son will miss you and wants to see what you're doing." (Teacher's answer: Umm, no.)

The gross awards:
- Don't lick the desk.
- Mask and pants up, please and thank you.
- Get your hand out of his butt crack.

Me: I feel like some of these might be timeless statements.
- Stop picking your nose with scissors (said to a 9th grader). Thankfully, the scissors were his.

State testing and the acronym nightmare:
- Because of NCLB (No Child Left Behind) we need to do well on the MSTEP (Michigan Student Test of Educational Progress), so let's have our PLC (Professional Learning Community) think of some great PBIS (Positive Behavioral Interventions and Supports) activities so that everyone can show what they've learned from the CCSS (Common Core State Standards).

Me: I had to look most of them up. I knew NCLB and PLC. I guessed Common Core, but didn't know the SS part, and MSTEP and PBIS had me stumped. To be fair, I don't work in Michigan, so that one was legitimately new to me.

Grading policies and late work:
- Of course, I'll accept 27 missing assignments on the last day of school. You know your social emotional health is more important than you learning responsibility.
- I will grade your work in purple ink because studies show that using red ink will hurt your feelings and make you feel inadequate.
- Of course, you didn't do well on the test, you didn't study nor pay attention in class and of course you can redo the test as many times as you want. I'll be happy to reteach you this after school on my own time even though you refused to do it the first time.

- You can do a retest and turn in anything late.
- Zeros are now weighted at 50%.

Me: Teachers control some of the grading policies, but things like 0's counting as 50's come down from on high.

(Lack of) Personal accountability:
- I'm so sorry I had to send you to the principal's office, for being disrespectful. I'm so glad they let you pick a prize out of the treasure box, before sending you back to class.
- Wow, you came to school today! Here is a gift card to McDonalds for your effort.

Social emotional health:
- The principal tells me that you are opting out of 5th grade math this year because it triggers you.
- Of course, everyone is first place.

Me: I find the sentiment admirable but the practice of *everyone's a winner* ultimately damaging. It encourages mediocrity.
- I'm sorry you are sad/angry/frustrated. Why don't you spend a few minutes in the Zen Den. Join us for our lesson when you feel ready to learn.

Me: Everybody has bad days and having supports for students can be a good thing. Teachers have no problems with the desire to support kids. However, a lack of personal accountability, discipline, and such actively hinders the ability to teach kids how to handle hard stuff.

Miscellaneous:
- I have to use my sick days to quarantine.

Closing thoughts and takeaways:
- These statements are a miniature look at some frustrations teachers have.

- While there is a focus on the negative, many students do fine, many policies do what they're supposed to, and most teachers love what they do.
- Loving what you do doesn't mean you agree with everything that happens at your job.
- Technology has made some major leaps and bounds. It's also inadvertently created some new things for teachers to deal with.

Chapter 57:
Episode 117 – Special Guest: Starting School During Covid – A Mother's Reflection

Introduction:

Dear Reader,

I'm going to break from tradition here and let this chapter stand largely on its own without much commentary from me.

That isn't me being lazy. This was presented to me as one mother's journal entry. It was her way of processing a difficult thing, and it stands well together as one entity.

~Ann

Dear Ann,

My daughter has always done things on her own schedule, and preparing for school was no different.

She potty trained late which delayed preschool, then Covid delayed things further.

Suddenly, any possibility of preschool was gone, and then, starting Kindergarten in the fall of 2020 was a minefield I was not prepared to navigate. So, starting school in person was delayed too.

I really thought I could get her prepared myself.

Kindergarten isn't required in our state, so I thought that with the help of ABC Mouse I could get my daughter ready to start first grade in the fall of 2021.

I was a part-time elementary substitute and then a special education para from 2006-2009, so I thought I had this covered. But there was one important difference—to my daughter, I will always be Mommy first, not her teacher.

When she got frustrated with a math game and I tried to get her to keep going, she pushed back.

She had tantrums that would rival any two or three-year-old, and she was six years old in December of 2020.

And the more often it happened, the more it wore me down, and I gave up too.

My attempt at an informal, go-at-her-own-pace homeschooling Kindergarten year was an epic failure, and I was afraid I'd made the wrong decision.

She would be turning seven in 2021, but she wasn't ready for first grade. So, I sent her to Kindergarten a year later than I would have if Covid hadn't interrupted our lives.

There was a brief introduction period over the summer—two weeks in June when my daughter could get to know her Kindergarten teacher and see what her school was like.

She cried when I left her, but it got better after the first day. I'm glad there was at least that small opportunity before diving headfirst into going to school for the first time.

School was from 9:15 to 4:00 Monday through Friday—no half-days for Kindergarten like I'd seen other schools doing in the past. The school I subbed at had half-day Kindergarten, but that was fifteen years ago, and things seemed to have shifted.

Kindergarten was now more like the way I remember first grade being, so in a way, it was good she was starting out older.

But in another way, it made things worse. The separation anxiety a four-year-old would go through for preschool was now happening to a six-and-a-half-year-old starting Kindergarten.

It started out okay because parents were allowed to come in with their children during the first week of school. We had breakfast together in the cafeteria, and I walked with her to her classroom. I don't remember there being any tears those first few days of school, and it looked like things were going to be okay.

But then I was called in to school to pick up my daughter because there was a confirmed exposure to another student with Covid.

That put us out of school and in quarantine for ten days.

Once it was time to go back to school, I made a map for my daughter to follow to her classroom since I couldn't go with her anymore.

The first day back went fine, but then her teacher took the map away and said she didn't need it. That seemed to trigger my daughter's anxiety, and the next few weeks were a mess of tears and my daughter saying she didn't want to leave me.

She cried on the way to school, cried when I left, and even tried to follow me out the door a few times. She also had to have someone walk her to her class.

I went home and cried too.

I tried so many different things to help my daughter with this transition, and nothing was working.

I was emotionally exhausted and resigned to waiting it out.

I knew she liked being at her school because she was always fine when I picked her up in the afternoon. Things finally got better when I decided to drive her to school in the morning. We live a couple blocks away and you can see our neighborhood from the playground, so it felt ridiculous to drive there, but it forced her to go in without me.

I couldn't wait around or I would hold up the car-rider line, and there were always attendants there to help move things along, so eventually she got used to going in without a fuss.

We played games in the car and had a fun routine going. She would still say, "But I'll miss you," but it was more like a part of our morning routine than an expression of not wanting to leave me.

I would remind her we would see each other after school, give her a kiss and a hug as she left, and everything was fine. Finally, a routine that worked.

So, despite the rocky start, the overall experience of my daughter's first year of school was a positive one. She loved her teacher and her classmates. My husband and I could tell how much being in school had helped her.

She even finished the year a little ahead of her grade level, which made me feel better about starting her a year later. Also knowing that there were other seven-year-olds in Kindergarten made me feel like I was not alone in the decision to wait.

We're all just doing the best we can and hoping it turns out okay. I feel confident that next year will be a lot smoother. It always helps to have a baseline experience when dealing with anxiety.

Takeaways:

- Everybody's school journey is different.
- Some roads are harder, but people adapt as needed.
- Experience can be a harsh but effective teacher.
- Sometimes, a change in routine can help a child's anxiety. In this case, it was a drive to school and a farewell ritual.
- The decision to wait or push a student ahead with others their age is one many families face. In most cases, there's no right or wrong answer. You do what works best for your family.

Chapter 58:
Episode 118 – General Opinion: Back to School Series – Advice for New Teachers Part 1

Introduction:

Dear Reader,

Throughout the series you got some of my advice for new teachers. Many of the special guests have also added their advice for people starting their teaching careers.

Chapter 15 talked about what the Overwhelmed New Teacher would look like, but it's about time to gather the info into one space anyway.

July is ending, and many schools start up again in August. My school won't begin until Labor Day, but we went well into June before halting for the summer.

~Ann

Disclaimer: There's a ton of advice out there. Some of it will probably contradict each other. Evaluate everything through the lens of your situation.

Source: These are drawn from social media posts. I will be paraphrasing.

Who is this Chapter for?
Whether a new or returning teacher, there's probably some great tips we can gather from the collective.

Parents may gain some insight into how to support their child's teacher.

Everybody. While many pieces of advice are specifically for First-Year Teachers, some have wider applications.

Advice I wouldn't/didn't take:
Please note that this does NOT make it bad advice. It just doesn't work with my personal preferences.

- Don't answer email outside of school hours.

Me: I do think having boundaries is excellent, but I'm a writer, emails are one of my favorite ways to communicate with parents. I really, really, really dislike phone conversations. At least with an email, I can proofread the response and run it past colleagues and friends.

- Run away.

Me: Most versions of this were said flippantly, but the question of whether it's the right career for you can only be answered by you. I'm just too darn stubborn to quit at this point.

- Never take work home.

Me: I do try to get a lot of grading done in school, but I also love to curl up on a couch and be comfortable if I have to grade. I've also gotten to the point where I spend all day some Saturdays to plan for the next three weeks to a month.

It may not be possible for a first-year teacher to keep work to work hours. You have a lot of extra stuff to do like come up with plans for the first time.

- Don't listen to other teachers about incoming students.

Me: I like to know how kids were and get a head's up if someone was particularly disruptive. Kids mature as they grow older. Even a few months can make a huge difference. I can't tell if a student has changed their ways if I don't know what their previous reputation was for comparison.

- Don't spend your own money.

Me: Definitely broke that one. I can use it for a small tax write off in my state, but that's beside the point. I spend my own money because I'm particular about the pens I get and the clipboard I use. I like having fun erasers for the kids to use. (The silly boys lose the privilege of animal head erasers when they start pelting each other with them.) I wanted a pencil sharpener that worked.

Pro tip: Do not leave the freshly sharpened pencils out. They will disappear never to be seen again. There is a slower leakage of pencils if they're not in sight.

Basically, most schools will provide you with supplies like pens and pencils, sticky pads of paper, looseleaf paper, and paper clips. That said, if you want a particular brand of pen or pencil, you're often on your own.

Sometimes, there's a reimbursement system. I don't bother, but if it matters to you, then go that route.

Interpersonal:
- Learn the kids' names, ask about their lives, and teach kindness through the practice of it.

Me: I struggle with names. Takes me like three weeks to learn the kids' names. I have them make nameplates so I can at least call on them by name from day one.

- Respect your students. That's the first step in having them respect you.
- Grow thick skin.
- Don't respond to emails angry.

Me: Emails are wonderful in that they can be ignored for a time. You're likely going to be thinking of the issue, whatever it may be until you answer it, but taking time away will let you answer more professionally. You may still want to tell the parent or administrator they're nuts and need to chill, but if you dash something off right away, you're more likely to stir up trouble.

- Don't let parents get to you.

Me: Being a great communicator will cut down on the number of negative parent interactions you have, but if you stick with teaching, you will have a conflict with a parent at some point. Make sure you document everything you can and pick the battles you want to fight.

- Don't let negative people get to you, including other teachers.

Me: The teaching career as a whole has some epic burnouts. Those in the process of burning out may just be perpetual sour-pusses.

- Be nice to secretaries and custodians.

Me: Agree. They often run the joint.

- Don't neglect yourself or your family.
- Leave your life choices and opinions at home. Stick to what you're supposed to teach. Keep a low profile.

Me: I hadn't considered this one. I mostly agree with it. Keep in mind that your worldview will shape who you are and how you interact with people. However, you were hired to teach, and you will have plenty of things to do your first year.

Shiny new teachers have lofty goals of changing the world. The world changing happens one kid at a time.

Classroom management:
- Make sure the students know you love them.
- Start classroom management from day one.
- Don't take it personally. Student behavior often has nothing to do with you.
- Show the kids you care.
- Treat every class like they're your favorite.

Me: Classes do have a personality. I think I struggle with this one, mostly because I'm not great at hiding feelings. If somebody's ticking me off, they're likely going to know it.

I work with high school kids though, so it's nicer to be able to tell them straight out they're being a pain and need to knock it off. Some listen. Some wander the classroom or lie on the floor. As long as they're not disturbing anybody in that moment (and they're safe), I don't care.

- Be firm, fair, and consistent.

Me: I would also add genuine to that list. The kids can (sometimes) sense if you're faking something.

- Building relationships with students does NOT mean being their friend.
- Keep high expectations for your students. No matter what's going on in their life outside the classroom, hold them accountable.

Me: Some school policies make that difficult but do your best. Even if students don't appreciate it now, accountability is one of those life lessons that pay off later.

Guess we should stop there. Lots more advice to come. Though practically the entire article is various takeaways, I'll highlight some of my favorites.

Takeaways:
- Be kind to people.
- Keep high expectations.
- Don't drown in negativity.
- Build relationships with students.

Chapter 59:
Episode 119 – General Opinion: Back to School Series – Advice for New Teachers Part 2

Introduction:

Dear Reader,

We're picking up right where we left off. I could have just thrown a giant list of advice at you, but I tried to break it into miniature themes.

~Ann

Disclaimer: Once again, I dug these tidbits from social media posts. I'm going to paraphrase most of them. I didn't read all the comments because they started to get repetitive.

Practical:

- Know the material inside and out. The confidence will show.

Me: Presumably, you enjoy learning if you choose to become a teacher. Let that joy shine through. Enthusiasm is addictive to some extent, especially in the lower grades. (It's a little harder to move teenagers unless your motivation is a phone or candy.)

- Be on time. Stay until you're supposed to.
- Be where you're supposed to be when you're supposed to be there. (I believe this refers to duties.)
- Clean yourself up and wash your hair. Dress appropriately. You're a professional.

Me: There may be a time when you're so overwhelmed that you can't make it to a duty without having a meltdown. In those cases, ask your supervisor or the principal if you can miss the duty. As long as you don't make a habit of it, most will grant the request.

- Participate in school spirit things if you can.
- Listen to veteran teachers.

Me: As with this list, you are likely to hear some contradictory statements. What's right will depend on your personality and your situation. Follow the advice that fits both best.

- Reflect.

Me: If you are willing to grow, the journey will be easier.

- Don't quit at the first sign of trouble. Trouble's coming in some way shape or form, but you entered the profession for a reason. Give yourself time to fairly evaluate whether it's the right fit for you.
- It's never too late to change your career. (There were several other *run away* comments.)

Me: Ha. I found those two pieces of advice right next to each other.

- Find someone at your school who loves the job and make them your go-to person.

Me: Teaching friends are important. Other friends are great too, but teaching friends usually come with spot-on empathy and a wicked sense of humor.

- Guard your heart and watch your back.

Me: People may let you down. There were also several comments on betrayal by students, colleagues, administration, and parents. I'm guessing there are some very specific stories behind those comments.

- You can use pre-made lessons.

Me: Most teachers are control freaks and modify the life out of any pre-made lesson, but it can be nice to start with something.

- Stick to contract time. Don't stay late at work.

Me: Personally, disagree. I prefer to do my grading and such at work. There are way less distractions for me. It's quiet after hours and before hours. People don't usually bother me, so I can get a lot done. Find the system that works for you.

- Don't be afraid to ask for help.

Me: This can be difficult. I once spent an hour trying to work up the nerve to ask somebody to grab a jug of milk for me because I was supposed to be quarantining.

- Give yourself the grace to make mistakes.
- Don't quit the career just because you lose one job. The school has to be right for you, just as you have to be a good fit for the school.

Me: I don't think anybody brings up that point enough. I've been in several schools. Each had its high points and problems. Every change I've made in district has always been for the better.

Factors that affect school fit aside:

- Salary
- Commute
- Schedule – i.e., how many classes you have, the student makeup of those classes, the number of students in your class that year
- Morale/atmosphere
- Colleagues/friends

Perspective:

- Celebrate success. Learn from mistakes.
- Much of student success is tied to how you treat them, not how you teach the curriculum.
- First year is the hardest. Remember that.
- You will be better next year.
- Everybody's just as overwhelmed and frustrated as you are.

Me: Not necessarily. First year is its own special brand of hard. Once you build enough lessons, you can adapt them. It's a heck of a lot easier to modify something than create it from scratch.

- Students will live up or down to your expectations.

Me: Oh, I like that one. It's also true. Seeking the easiest road is just human nature.

- Fulfill your contract. The powers that be don't care how loyal you've been. Do what's best for you and your students.

Inspirational:

- Just do your best. It will be good enough.
- Don't expect to be a perfect teacher.
- Learn to adapt and embrace change.

- Don't get so busy making a living that you forget to live.

Unique:
- Make a scrap book.

Me: Cool if it works for you. Personally, I have too much paperwork already. Scrapbooking doesn't relax me.

- Keep the little thank you cards and notes kids give you in a drawer to lift your spirits on a bad day.

Staying sane:
- You do not need to grade everything.

Me: Oh, that's good advice. It's also very difficult for me to implement. I often go over answers or have kids switch papers and grade something then just mark it as participation.

- Learn to say, "No."

Me: That is a whole heap harder than it sounds. It can be difficult to navigate what is acceptable in terms of extra work and legitimate take-one-for-the-team tasks and what's outright crappy work practices.

- Make the most of in-school time.
- Pick and choose what gets done.

Me: Trying to do it all will burn you out.

- Set boundaries.
- If you need to cry, do it.
- Work is work. Home is home. Keep it that way.
- Get mental health supports in place before the crazy hits.
- Routines! They'll save you time. They'll save your voice.
- Make sure you get your me time. Schedule in free time for yourself if you have to.

- Do NOT take any unpaid extra jobs (if you can help it). Schools will take advantage of the eager-to-impress attitude.

My advice:

- Go to sporting events, concerts, and school plays. It's fun and fulfilling to see the kids outside the classroom.
- Use the restroom when you can. Eat when you can. Teaching's one of those professions where sometimes you can't just leave to do what you want when you want because you're responsible for others.

Takeaways:

- Classroom routines will help with managing student behavior and keeping you sane. And that's really a main goal here.
- Never underestimate the power of a good cry.
- Set boundaries with work in general, students, parents, and administration.
- Eat, drink, and use the facilities when you can.

Chapter 60:
Episode 120 – General Opinion: Back to School Series – Advice for New Teachers Part 3 (Best School Supplies)

Introduction:

Dear Reader,

While I agree with the sentiment that teachers shouldn't be required to purchase their own supplies, I've also become something of a pen snob. (I use G2 Pilot .7 pens in fun colors. They're generally very reliable, though it's difficult to find the teal color. It's like the light blue but better.)

Herein, you will likely see way more than you ever wanted to of what I buy for my classroom and why.

Confession: I'm also one of those people who enjoys shopping for school supplies. I'll wander into a grocery store for milk and come out with some stickers and sticky note pads (because you literally cannot have enough of those in fun colors.)

Today, I was in a Walmart for an electric skillet and happened to come out with mechanical pencils. They were pretty and affordable!

Because I didn't want this to be all about me, I'm also including some random answers from social media.

~Ann

Why would teachers buy their own supplies?
- The school supplies an inferior quality item.
- School district can't afford additional supplies.
- Item not covered by what the school supplies to the teachers.
- Personal preference – This is probably the most popular reason.
- Teacher is addicted to buying school supplies. (*Raises hand. Guilty.)
- More convenient – Not going to lie, this is probably my go-to reason for most purchases. In many schools, the school would buy something if you had the foresight to place it on the order the previous year.

What kind of supplies do teachers buy? (Doubles as my personal shopping list.)
- Candy – Jolly Ranchers, Nerds, Laffy Taffy, Dum Dums
- Snacks – chips and other snack packs

Me: Yes, those count as school supplies to me because they are for use at school. In particular, I buy some sort of granola bar in case I get called to cover a class during the time I would normally be eating. I get lightheaded and grumpy if you don't feed me regularly, and nobody wants that. I also stock chips and candy. (Chocolate and such for me and my teaching buddies and Dum

Dums or other low-risk-of-allergy type candy for the kiddos.)

- Erasers
- Low-Pressure Stapler – I bought one of the low-pressure staplers. If you have to staple 100 papers together because you forgot that setting on the copier, you're gonna want this.
- Tissues – The school I work for has tissues, but I prefer getting the giant box Kleenex ones from Costco.
- Stickers
- Sharpies in fun colors
- Cardstock – I use it a lot for projects.
- Hand sanitizer – The school had giant containers of stuff that smelled like rotting coconuts. I'd rather just have the kids use the normal type that just smells like alcohol.
- Cleaning wipes – It's always nice to be able to pretend your desk is germ free for a hot second.
- Electric pencil sharpener – I have two. Might be replacing one of the ones that isn't working too well, but sometimes, it's not the machine that's not working, it's the kid not knowing how to work the machine. Some pencil sharpeners have quirks like over sharpens one side, so you need to press down slightly or rotate the pencil to get it evenly sharp.
- Calculators – certain subjects
- Writing implements – highlighters, pens, pencils
- Lined paper/composition notebooks
- Two-pocket folders

Most awesome school supplies ever purchased: That's a stretch but I get it:
- Booze – And no, you cannot bring it to school but from a certain point of view, it might be considered a school

supply.

Essentials:
- #2 Pencils or mechanical pencils – kids lose them constantly; it's always good to have spares around
- Post-it Notes – fun colors
- Pencil holder – I use a Star Wars toothbrush holder and a mug I cracked.
- Electric pencil sharpener – If you can only get one thing, this is it.

Electronics (and ways to deal with them):
- Timer
- Amazon echo
- Microsoft Surface Pro with remote access to LDC projector/ laptop
- Keurig or other coffee maker
- Document camera
- Cell phone pocket holder
- Standing baskets/ some way to organize student headphones
- Laser pointer – probably outside the scope of what most schools supply

Mood setting and indicating:
- Diffuser – Check your school's policy on this first. It's generally not a great idea to get things with heavy scents because kids are allergic to the world.
- A lamp – makes the room feel homier
- My Last Nerve Plushie
- Stuffed animals – even high schoolers love something cuddly
- Soft lights; fairy lights (Christmas lights)

Larger and larger ticket items:
- Laminator – I had gotten one to review. I think the office has bigger and better ones, but the little one works fine in a pinch.
- Microwave
- Refrigerator
- Small white boards
- Smart board
- Rolling cart
- HP printer with instant ink
- Whiteboard
- Step ladder – I just climb lab counters, but step ladders are nice too.
- Paper cutter – My school has some spiffy ones by some of the copiers, but I can definitely see the appeal of getting one if that wasn't the case.
- Free standing easels
- Stand up desk
- Dictionary – unabridged
- Dish washer – School should have that in the science prep rooms.
- Dorm furniture

Random:
- Books
- Pool noodles

Me: Wait, what? Why?

- Braille embosser
- Cordless hot glue gun
- Jenga and other games
- Skeletons – plastic ones!

- Knick knack – student gifts
- Books on classroom management
- Goat bell to summon kids from recess
- A pumpkin that got adopted by the class
- Segmented worm toy – surprisingly popular
- Math clock – has math symbols instead of numbers
- Bean bags – I have some, but I don't think I'm going to leave those out on the desk.
- Scratch Off stickers – You write your own reward underneath and place the sticker on top.

Me: I want them! Never thought of this one. Forget school. I'm buying these for me.

- Fish tank – Not for me, but if you're willing to care for fish, they can be a nice addition to a classroom.
- Room freshener – People in large groups (and most middle school age children) are stinky.

What do you do if you want something but can't afford to buy it?

- Make an Amazon wish list.
- Ask around your social media circles.
- Look around on free cycle and garage sales.
- Ask your school administrators if they will buy it for you.
- Try one of the Gofundme type online crowd funding endeavors for school supplies.

Closing comments:

From what I gather, especially from the random list, you should fill your classroom with stuff that reflects your personality. I have a colleague who has Funko pop toys and video game posters around.

I put an educational Star Wars poster up. I also have random Star Wars toys hanging about my room.

You will spend a lot of time in school. Sometimes, you'll want a space you can retreat to where you can rest and recharge.

Takeaways:
- Electric pencil sharpeners are awesome.
- If you can't afford something, ask around.
- If you can afford it, there are many fun supplies that will make your teaching life much easier.

To Be Continued …

Thank You for Reading:

Dear Reader,

This book would never have happened without the Vella program.

Special thanks to everybody who agreed to do interviews.

Schools have all kinds of stakeholders. Each person has a vested interest in seeing students succeed. It's been interesting to hear from some of the many perspectives out there.

There is much more to come. Stay tuned for Volume 3.

If you'd like to keep up with my work, email **devyaschildren@gmail.com** and/or sign up for my newsletter on my website. (**juliecgilbert.com**)

Sincerely,

Ann Y. Mouse
(Julie C. Gilbert)

Love Science Fiction or Mystery?

Choose your adventure!

Visit: **http://www.juliecgilbert.com/**

For details on getting free books

www.ingramcontent.com/pod-product-compliance
Lightning Source LLC
LaVergne TN
LVHW051224080426
835513LV00016B/1388